Pathwork
2nd Editi

By Pete Jennings & Pete Sawyer

ISBN 1 898307 00 8

Pathworking
2nd Edition

©1993 Pete Jennings & Pete Sawyer

ALL RIGHTS RESERVED

Published by:

Capall Bann Publishing
Freshfields
Chieveley
Berks
RG16 8TF

About the authors

Pete Jennings and Pete Sawyer originally met during 1990 in Ipswich and found a common interest in Pathworking. Both had previously practiced it with others as well as solo, but as no local group existed, they decided to form one. The group grew and has had to be split a couple of times to keep the numbers manageable, with the original students becoming able to now organise their own groups.

Invariably, the various participants asked where they could read more about pathworking and to answer this apparent gap in the publishing world, the two decided to write one, which is the origin of this book.

Both are pagans, (Jennings of the Northern Tradition and Sawyer of the Celtic), but the book they produced should be of value whatever your religious beliefs.

Originally from London, Pete Sawyer works in local government and is an experienced and excellent Tarot reader. Pete Jennings splits his time between broadcasting for the BBC, writing, lecturing and editing the Pagan magazine Gippeswic. He reads Runes as well as Tarot and is an organiser of various folk and Pagan activities in his native Suffolk.

Foreword

In this book we try to fill an apparent gap in the range of material available on esoteric subjects. It is designed to be a practical book, so you will not find thousands of footnotes and academic crossreferences. You will however find plenty of practical help in setting up sessions, with a good cross section of scenarios to try. In following the book you will also learn how to construct your own paths and Chapter 8 gives some more advanced examples. We originally published this book ourselves to fulfil the needs of the many people who asked us 'where is the book to read up on this?'. Having failed to find one, we wrote it ourselves, based on several years of practical experience between us. Since that original edition, we have made some additions and clarifications and the whole thing has been reset for a more legible read in candlelight by a 'proper' publisher.

Pathworking, which is sometimes referred to as channelling or questing, is used by many different groups, from New Age followers trying to raise their consciousness to Pagans attempting healing rituals. One doesn't have to possess any particular beliefs, or large sums of money to benefit from it, and it can be conducted within a group or solo, at time intervals to suit you, and not to a vigorous pattern. The chances are though that once you get into it you'll feel you are 'missing out' if you are unable to pathwork once a week. It is safe, cheap and takes no more skill than an open minded attitude. It can relieve every day stress, improve your conception of yourself and the world around you, and help you resolve both practical and spiritual problems.

We would like to thank members of our Ipswich Pathworking Group who were very often the first to try these paths and evaluate them. Their suggestions and encouragement is much appreciated. Pathworking can be both highly entertaining and relaxing, so read on and enjoy!

Pete Jennings & Pete Sawyer 1993

What is Pathworking?

In essence, pathworking is a method of going on meditational journeys. What those journeys consist of and how they are achieved is largely up to the participant, but in this book we are trying to provide a Do-It-Yourself blueprint to enable anyone to start from scratch and achieve results.

Undoubtedly along the way you will discover other methods and refinements to the process we describe. They will probably be no more right or wrong than the ones we describe, as there aren't really any hard and fast rules. However all the methods and scenarios we use have been successfully field tested within our own groups, so they make a very good base to start from.

To pathwork, one must first alter ones state of consciousness so that you are receptive to what is happening. Educationalists have long recognised the beneficial effects of learning things just before one drops off to sleep, or even during it as in under- pillow tape players. The brain seems to accept messages easier and at a deeper level when the information is contained subliminally. This has even been recognised in law, where subliminal advertising messages are prohibited from films and t.v. (this is where an image is flashed for just one frame and the brain registers it even though it is over before one consciously notices it.

Pathworkers tend to use several methods simultaneously to alter consciousness and we will discuss them in details in later chapters, but briefly, sound, smell and relaxation techniques are all employed. Some may even use drugs or alcohol, but these are unnecessary and potentially harmful, or even illegal.

Once the consciousness has been changed (it is hard to define whether it is higher or lower because that depends ones definitions) a scene is set in which to travel.

This scene is usually worked out in advance and will depend on what one is trying to achieve, i.e. relaxation, problem solving, enlightenment, healing, spiritual growth, entertainment etc.

This scene is usually worked out in advance, and will depend on what one is trying to achieve eg. Relaxation, problem solving, enlightenment, healing, spiritual growth, entertainment etc.

Spoken descriptions are progressively trimmed down from a detailed initial location to a sparsely sketched in situation which is interactive with the participants thoughts. Eventually, the participant will be left to develop their own continuing role and situation, before being brought back to reality. Before being brought back it is usual to include a healing sequence that leaves one feeling better than when one started.

A short period of readjustment and collection of thoughts is normally allowed before the success or otherwise of the working is analysed. If the pathworking is to be successful this should never be rushed, with each member of a group being given their say in turn, with the rest of the group in a supportive role. Of course, sometimes someone will wish to keep their adventures secret, and this should be respected also so as not to cause embarrassment. If working solo it should be remembered that this part is as important as all the others if one is to derive the maximum benefit from a session.

It is a good discipline, whether one works solo or in a group to keep a simple diary of what was carried out. Not only will you be able over a period to discern patterns and methods particularly successful for you, but the process of writing down will make it more real and permit yourself further analysis.

In an ideal world one could use a combination of working both solo and within groups, but this is not always practical. It is usually easier to learn the techniques within a group first, even if you are all at the beginning stage together. Having said that one must chose ones company wisely, and it is better to try working alone than attempting to relate to individuals with ulterior motives for running a group. Whatever you do, try not to rush into it blindly. Take the time to read the book more than once if you need to (it doesn't cost any more!) and seriously consider what you want to get out of it. Do you want it purely as a way of getting rid of stress, or have you some spiritual needs? With the emphasis on creative visualisation within Wiccan (witchcraft) ranks nowadays it could be a useful way of developing a personal tool, but it could as well be a means of solving problems for members of any of the more orthodox religions. Whatever you want from it be warned! - you only get out what you put in, so prepare carefully.

2. HOW TO PREPARE FOR A PATHWORKING SESSION.

Easier said than done when in pathworking you expect the unexpected! In practical terms though it is a matter of eliminating distractions. That is dealt with in chapter 5, so lets get down to the more important matter of preparing yourself. Presuming it is a group working you are preparing for, start by considering who is going to be there, and what their needs are. Invariably, some of those needs will clash. Sometimes that can be resolved by incorporating more than one element into your scenario, but you may also consider doing two separate workings in the same session or catering for different groups at different times. Do not forget your own needs too. It is good to give a pleasant pathworking to a group, but if you fail to look after your own needs you will eventually lose your enthusiasm. The group owe it to you to make sure that you enjoy the experience too, either by working elements in to please yourself, or by someone else taking charge occasionally. Chapter 7 gives many example scenarios for you to work on, and should give you the ideas for formulating your own.

You should be relaxed and happy within yourself. Sort out practical problems before the day when you can, so as not to have them simmering on the back burner of your mind. If you cannot sort them out, identify clearly what they are so that you can specifically deal with them during the pathworking. Always try the practical approach to problems first though, by talking to that doctor/ lawyer/accountant/shop assistant/colleague or lover, rather than using what should be a good experience as an emotional crutch. (Make sure this applies to your group members also!).

Set a realistic time for the session to start, and stick to it. Make it late enough for you to have travelled, worked, eaten, watched a favourite t.v. programme etc. without rushing. If possible, sit quietly, thinking about what you are aiming to do before you start opening the door to your visitors. Make it clear to them beforehand that if they are not there by an agreed time the session will start without them. This is very important, as a session should never be disturbed once it has begun. Make sure you have all got the gossip, cigarettes and going to the loo out of the way before you begin. Also make sure that your projected working will leave enough time at the end for every one to describe and analyse what they have done before the last bus leaves.

When everyone is settled (see chapter 5 for setting a room), an informal, easy but quiet atmosphere should be encouraged. Make a deliberate act of lighting candles and incense and starting the music. This should remind the pathworkers to get in the right frame of mind, to cease chattering and fidgeting and to start their relaxation exercises.

Newcomers should be introduced and made to feel welcome, and it should be explained that no one will be pressured into talking about their experiences afterwards unless they are willing. It should also be mentioned that in the unlikely event of someone being in a situation they dislike during the pathworking, they have only to open their eyes and they will be back to reality. Also, in deference to the others,if anyone fails to 'go down', they should must remain quiet and still until the others have finished. It should be pointed out that there is no shame in this, and happens to everyone at sometime or other.

THE RELAXATION TECHNIQUE

After re-assuring any newcomers what sort of thing you are about to do (without giving away the 'plot') and that this is safe, the first thing to establish is that everyone is sitting or lying comfortably within the room. Wear loose informal clothing, kick off your shoes and stretch out. Talk everyone through relaxation in a set order. A favourite way is to say something like "Your toes and feet are warm and relaxed. All the aches of the day are draining out of them into the carpet. Now feel that warmth and relaxation spreading up your body into your legs, as your eyes close."

All this should be said in a deep, low, calm voice. THIS IS EXTREMELY IMPORTANT. This type of voice should be used throughout the pathworking, and should be unexcited without lapsing into monotone. Now would be a good time, in that same tone of voice, to start the simultaneous breathing exercise. This increases oxygen into the bloodstream, and flushes out stale air from the unused corners of your lungs. Instruct the group to breathe in deeply through the nose, and hold it, (for 5 - 10 seconds). Now instruct them to exhale fully, through their open mouths. These instructions should be repeated frequently until the group is audibly breathing together.

The relaxation instructions can now be extended further up the body eg. "The rosy glow is spreading its healing into your knees, thighs, hips etc...and so on through the chest, arms and finally the head. While you are doing this you must continue to monitor that the deep breathing is continuing. If it is not, reintroduce some short instructions such as "breathing in now...hold it..and out" until the pattern is restored.

When you reach the head, reinforce some idea of control and security by saying something along the lines of "Your eyes are so heavy that you wouldn't want to open them. All is safe and calm as we look at the scene before us, accompanied by our friends within this room. Just let the music fill you ears, and a kind, blue healing light fill your vision, blocking out all other thoughts." Leave a gap here to let the group come to terms with the new situation. It will also give you time to catch up with the rest of the groups state, and gather your thoughts before setting the scene, which we deal with next.

3. SETTING A SCENARIO

Before setting a scenario, several factors should be taken into consideration:

a)   The people for whom it is to work

b)   The objects which it must set out to achieve eg. Entertainment, spiritual development, healing, relaxing, problem solving, stress management. (Incidentally notice I use the phase stress management. Most of us need, indeed enjoy, a small amount of stress - it gets the adrenalin going! However, some people get more of their fair share of it, whether it be at work or in the home. It is the balancing out of this we should seek to redress, not its cancellation.

c)   Whether you need an entirely different time or place to the ones previously used, or whether you wish to carry on from them.

d)   Whether you need to avoid certain situations. It is not a good idea to put your group onto the roof of the Empire State Building if one of them is terrified of heights - unless you are intending to do this as part of their therapy!

e)   Whether you need to go back to a very simple format to allow some newcomers to come in gently, rather than being pitched into a more advanced model.

f)   Can the plot be synchronised with the changes in the music available, and is that music long enough and of the right type?

When you have taken all these factors into consideration you can begin to rough out your plot. Full plot scenarios can be found in chapters 7 and 8, but they follow the same general structure. This should fall into four sections ie.

1. Getting down - scene setting.

In this you find a way to alter the groups state of consciousness eg. Going down 10 stone steps, one at a time. At this stage you need to paint a very vivid picture, describing the walls, the stonework arches etc. This tends to block out any residue images left in the minds of the participants, as they consider these details. If done successfully, they should then be in a calm, non - fidgeting state, with a slowed pulse rate and steady breathing. This breathing will not be so deep as the initial rate set up. This should lead naturally onto section 2.

2. The action plot.

Initially this will contain the same amount of detail, eg Describe walking down a corridor and into a room. The plot now switches to more generalised details, eg. "There is a table in the room with something on it". Note that the age and type of table and room have not been described. That is for the individuals to visualise themselves. Most will see something different and unique to them. Sometimes though you will be surprised to find that two or more pathworkers will get the same type of symbolism independently.

You can then tell them something along the lines of "pick it up and examine it. Explore the room and I will return for you in a little while." Everyone will then develop the plot in their own way, and you can too, so long as you are remaining aware of what is going on outside of this. For instance, is anyone in distress? Check occasionally by opening your eyes and watching for signs of extreme restlessness. If this should happen (and it is quite rare) bring the whole group up in a short version of section 4. Usually though, people are able to either just open their eyes, or just 'think' themselves into another situation.

As you become more experienced you will find that you can quite easily dip in and out of the working to for instance register what stage the music is at. This is another factor that must be monitored, and it helps if you have listened to the piece privately beforehand to get to know it. When you feel that you have explored the situation properly, you must gently interrupt the others before moving them on. Remember they may be at different stages to you, and may be reluctant to progress on, so your voice must be firm. You can then if you wish take the plot further, e.g. Turn the participants to birds, so that they can fly out of the room, with another free form section for them to fill in themselves. When you have finished the plot which you had previously planned though, move on to section 3.

3. The healing process.

This ensures that the participants come back feeling better than when they went away. You could for instance describe a healing waterfall under which they stand and have all their aches and tensions washed away. Of course there are lots of other alternatives that you can get from chapters 7 and 8, such as rays of light etc., or you can come up with some of your own. When this has been completed (and it could even contain a suggestion such as "cigarettes will taste nasty to Mary when she returns" to help someone kick the habit) it is time to finish on section 4.

4. The return to reality.

This returns everyone back to their normal mental state, and should be done gently but thoroughly. You should announce the intention to return, and it is usually best, (though it can be done in different ways) to reverse the process of section 1. So if you came down 10 steps, one at a time, reverse that by going up them, one at a time. Finally, tell everyone to open their eyes when ready. If anyone is reluctant to come back up, call them again.

People have such a good time that they are occasionally reluctant to return. Avoid any sudden shocks when people return. Keep the room candlelit and do not switch on the electric light just yet until they are ready. Do not let the music cut off suddenly. Gently fade it down with the volume control if necessary. Let everyone adjust back gradually without firing questions at them or bustling about. You will now be ready to discuss and analyse what has happened, which we cover in the next chapter.

4. ANALYSING THE PATHS TAKEN

You may want to serve refreshments now, but personally I prefer to wait until afterwards, as you cannot stop the others discussing whilst you are busy in the kitchen. It helps if you go round the room from a different point or person each time, so that the same people are not always first or last. Be sensitive to the fact that not everyone may wish to discuss things in public. Also make sure that each participant speaking can be heard by everyone present, and that reasonable order is kept. There can often be hilarity at this point, but it should never be at the cost to the speakers feelings. Anyone who hasn't managed to get down should be reassured that it happens to us all. It may help to identify why they think it never worked for them this time, (eg stressful day at work, uncomfortable chair etc) so that the problem may be better dealt with by you the next time.

Some people may be entirely adequate at divining their own meanings, others may benefit from advice and suggestions by the group as a whole. People do tend to see things in terms of their own personal experiences, so recent reading or viewing material will often make its presence felt. Some symbology may be obscure to all, and the pathworker may have to ask questions within another pathworking to decipher the meaning. Books on dream interpretation can be useful although some of them can be over fanciful with no apparent factual basis. Of course, for some of the lighter, more entertaining workings there is no real message other than to enjoy yourself, and there is nothing wrong with that.

It is always dangerous to jump to conclusions on meanings, but my advice is always to trust to immediate gut reaction rather than being ruled by the more literary or intellectual outpourings.

5. FORMING A GROUP AND SETTING UP A ROOM

The type of group
One must consider carefully before you leap into forming a pathworking group, as it carries a commitment in time and effort, and a responsibility for what the members get out of it. We believe however that groups are the best way to get into pathworking, so if one doesn't exist, you are probably going to have to form it yourself. Some forethought here will save a great deal of trouble later.

Firstly, you must consider why you are doing it. Is it to be a mutual self help affair, with members taking turns to lead workings or a commercial proposition with you charging for a service given? If it is a self help affair, you may be able to rotate sessions round various members homes, with them providing hospitality on a rota basis. However, not everyone has a suitable room, so it may be that others could contribute in other ways by supplying biscuits, candles, tapes etc. If you do take this route, you must be careful that members contribute equally. If this is a problem, it is a better idea to charge a subscription with the hosts taking expenses out of the central fund.

The room
If it is to be a commercial affair, then you need to sort out a budget for yourself before you start, so that the charge you make is realistic to cover all expenses plus something for your own time. If you have a suitable and large enough room fine, but if not you are going to have to find somewhere that is quiet, warm, accessible with no possibility of interruption from outside sources. This isn't always easy! Easy chairs should be used for preference, although some people prefer to use cushions or bean bags on the floor to relax on. Windows need to be adequately curtained, and either a locked or bolted door barring access. If there is a telephone in the room, it needs to be of the type where the ringer can be switched off, or an ansaphone fitted. Doorbells need to be disabled too, once your guests are in.

Within the room, it is best if the seating can be arranged in a rough circle, with a low table in the middle and plenty of leg and elbow room. On the table you can place a candle, in a suitable holder and your source of incense. This can be either of the joss stick variety, with a suitable ash catcher, or an oil evaporator. (In these a candle is lit beneath a small reservoir of water and aromatic oil, which evaporates into the room.) Charcoal type incense burners tend to be a bit unsuitable in confined spaces. The type of incense that you use is really up to personal taste, but try avoiding anything too strong. Something like white musk is ideal. If you collect donations for the evening, a small container for these can also be left on the table.

The music

The person leading the pathworking will need to be at that point around the circle where the hi-fi or cassette player is situated. The sound should be controlled easily by use of the volume control or alternatively by the more modern remote control, but don't forget that you will have to operate in semi-darkness. The level should be kept quite low whilst speaking, and brought up slightly in the free form sections. There are thousands of 'New Age' type music tapes and CDs around, so the choice is yours. In choosing your sounds though, bear a few points in mind:

a)   Is the sound suitable for the plot? It is disconcerting hearing the sound of the sea when you are supposed to be flying over mountain tops.

b)   Does the sound penetrate deep enough? Some tapes have too many high trilling notes and not enough low, bass ones. We always prefer an occasional deep, almost sub sonic bass to be heard frequently. The tempo should also be quite slow.

c)   Do not repeat the same track too often, unless you specifically wish to invoke an experience triggered by it before. Rotate your sounds round. You needn't even have music. Why not try one of whale sounds or of a running stream instead? These are available too. Why not create your own tape by recording some natural sounds interspersed with tracks from various sources? The possibilities are endless.

d)   Can you get your plot changes to synchronise in with the track changes? Rehearse beforehand, and make sure that the track lengths are right for what you intend to do while they are playing.

e)   You should be aware of the music as part of the background. It should help to block out external noises such as dogs barking, traffic and domestic appliances. If you notice the music too much during the actual pathworking it is likely to be for one of the following reasons:

   i)   You are using the same track too frequently.
   ii) The music is being played too loud or distorted.
   iii) The music is unsuitable for the plot.
   iv) The music composition is unsuitable eg. too fast /shrill/aggressive etc.
   v)   You are not getting deep enough down into the subconscious for other reasons. eg Stressed / cold /uncomfortable etc.

Recruiting your members

O.K., so you have the room, the music, candles, incense and armed with this book, the knowledge, but who do you pathwork with? If you have some sympathetic, like minded friends fine, but if not you are in one way or another going to have to advertise. Yes, that can be a dirty word to some, but if you are going to find others it is crucial, so you might as well get it right to find suitable people.

If you are a member of a New Age organisation or something like the Pagan Federation, no problem, as you can generally make contact (often for free) via newsletters. Even if you are not a member of those sorts of organisations, special interest magazines often carry a modestly priced personal ad. column, frequently with box numbers. We would always recommend the use of box numbers, as it allows you the luxury of vetting applicants without revealing your own identity and address.

The content of the advertisement is of course up to you, but be advised not to make wild claims for Pathworking that you cannot necessarily produce. Try and keep things in general terms, without targeting any specific interest group and you will more likely get a wider range of ages, interests and geographic locations. You can of course use such an advertisement in your local press, and if you do not mind "going public" might even persuade them to run an article about it. Press advertisements can be expensive though, so do not forget that you can often put a small poster up at the library or even the shop where you buy your candles, incense and tapes from! If you wish to remain semi anonymous, why not just put a contact telephone number, without a name or address? Similarly, some people who would wish to reply will want to be reassured that their confidentiality will be maintained, so why not include a phrase to the effect of "Discretion assured and expected in return."

Once you have your replies, how do you deal with them? Promptly is the one word answer. There is nothing more frustrating than waiting for a reply to a box numbered ad. when you have no way of knowing if your letter even reached it. Even if it is only a brief acknowledgement to let them know you will be interviewing soon, it takes the urgency out of the situation. You can even make a request in the ad. for a stamped, self addressed envelope to be forwarded, into which you can return fuller details in writing.

We advise setting up interviews in a neutral (eg cafe, pub) place, with one individual at a time. This way, if you are not happy that they would fit in to a group, they have no way of badgering you at your undisclosed address or telephone number. You should be looking out for the following factors:

    i)   Are they open minded and honest?
    ii)   Do they seem to have a genuine interest?
    iii) Will their social status fit in with the rest of the group? (A tricky one this - you will have to decide whether you want a mixed variety of people or all of a similar class and type).

iv) Do they have an ulterior motive for coming? e.g. To meet others and possibly recruit them for their particular interest.
v) Will they be able to attend regularly and on time?
vi) Are they able to offer anything to the group in return, such as alternative premises?
vii) Will they be sensitive to the needs of others within the group? Someone who is very talkative, opinionated, rude or pedantic may upset the balance and harmony you wish to encourage. It is better to lose one person at this stage than lose several others because of them later.

As always, go on gut reactions. We are far better at judging people like this than we sometimes imagine. If you are a student of body language, do not forget to use the valuable insights that this gives you as well.

It is only fair that in interviewing others they should also ask questions of you, so do go prepared with the details you wish to divulge at this stage. If the interview is successful, you may like to invite the candidate to try things for one trial week, where they can see if it suits them while the group finds out the same in return. When the group is established, you may feel that it is o.k. for existing members to bring along newcomers on the same basis without prior consultation. The group can then democratically decide afterwards whether they are willing for them to return at subsequent sessions. Alternatively, you may wish to retain control of this aspect, but do not forget the feelings of the others when deciding to allow a stranger into their homes and be privy to their thoughts and emotions. You must also at this time compile a record of names, addresses and telephone numbers, in case a session has to be suddenly cancelled or moved. Otherwise, records and formality can be relaxed as you like within a self help group, but if you are providing a service for money, it is a job like any other and subject to income tax etc. You will then need to keep all receipts and details of income.

One final word of warning! Although group pathworking can bring much joy, occasionally it can bring sadness too, especially when members get insights into things they would sometimes rather not know. It is worth making this point at the initial interview. It is also worth remembering that you are not a trained social worker, and should know when to advise your new found friends where to seek further professional help when necessary, rather than try adhoc counselling of your own. Beware the perpetual lame duck who tries to you use you and the group as a crutch, instead of as a means of developing themselves and solving problems from within.

THE VIKING VALKNUT

A powerful sigil which symbolises the interconnection between the nine worlds, a highly significant number in Norse religion (3 times 3). Why not try using it as the basis for a solo pathworking, using some of the information from later in the book? (See path 31)

6. SOLO PATHWORKING

As we have said before, it is easier to pathwork within a group. However, you can also use similar techniques on your own. Maybe it is impractical for you to join or set up a group. Alternatively, you may be part of a group but wish to experience some alternative, different scenarios away from it.

This need particularly applies to witches, or wiccans to give them their correct name. It should be emphasised though that doing solo pathworkings does not make you a witch, and you can do them and still be a member of most religions, or no religion at all. If you are going to use pathworking (solo or group) for occult purposes though, it is as well to protect yourself within a magic circle first, and to remember that any harmful thing attempted will rebound on you three-fold. As well as wicca, solo pathworkings are often used for shamanistic journeys. Sometimes the shaman (or more often his assistant) will beat a drum to help induce the trance state, and often enters the 'other' world by the same entrance. Wiccans and shamen sometimes use natural haluciogenics to aid them, but these must be viewed with caution, as they are often poisonous in wrong dosage.

The use of pathworking within wiccan and shamanistic circles will probably form the basis of a future book by us, as it is outside of the scope of beginners. However, some simple working examples have been included in Chapter 8 for information. We have also included a list of some useful books in the bibliography at the back.

When working alone, you can be very specific about what path you want to take, so take the time to plan carefully. Having said that, you must allow space for you to react within the situation you find yourself in. You can set up a room just like in chapter 5, but you could just as easily use the privacy of your bedroom if you sleep alone. Set up your music, candle and incense in there and you can be ready to go. You will need to concentrate hard to put yourself through the relaxation and breathing exercises already described, but you can of course take things at your own pace. Do not rush things though. Indeed, one of the joys of solo pathworking is that you can afford the luxury of time to go down really deep. Which brings us neatly on to the biggest problem of solo pathworking - coming back up.

You are likely to enjoy yourself and be unaware of time. So you need a reliable way to stop yourself. You can give yourself an instruction at the start that you must return when the music stops, but for some people that has the same effect as an alarm clock (which can also be used) - it is heard but ignored. A more effective solution can be to incorporate a fast, jangling piece of music at the end of the tape (or even to have a second tape that fires off in those twin tape deck systems.) If you are really good you can rely on pure willpower, but don't blame us for missed appointments!

When you do come back up be sure to scribble down the details of what you have experienced, especially if it is late at night and the bed looks inviting. You will have lost most of the detail, (and its use in further analysis) by morning.

7. SIMPLE SCENE SETTING

Each of the following scenarios have been used successfully in the past, and can work for you to. By working through a few as they stand you should get the general idea. In the early ones we have annotated the sections 1 - 4 , as per the description in Chapter 3. To remind you briefly they are: 1. Getting down - scene setting. 2. The action plot. 3. The healing process. 4. The return to reality. Some of the plots are very simple. These are often some of the best, and can produce a very wide range of responses from within a group. As you become more experienced, you might like to 'mix-and-match' sections from different workings together, or add several action plots simultaneously together in the middle to form a longer one. You will need to create a bridging sequence within them, as it isn't very comfortable to be whipped from one scene to another without some sort of link. Most of the workings given last approximately 25 - 35 minutes. You will find in practice this seems longer or shorter than it really is. As you will be doing this in semi-darkness, you will need to part memorise the gist of the story (although not the actual words) before you go down. You will find in practice, however hard you prepare the plot, it always seems to take on a life of its own in the telling. Details will be added, changed or lost. Do not worry about this, as it is perfectly natural for your subconscious intuition to take over. Don't fight it - you will invariably find that it enhances and enriches the experience.

Don't forget before you do 'go down' to secure the room and telephone, get the incense, candle and music going and make sure everyone is in a relaxed state. Start the relaxation and breathing exercises in that deep, calm voice and enjoy yourselves. (See chapter 2 if you are still not sure how to do this.)

PATH No. 1
A nice easy basic one to get you started

(1)   As you relax and breathe deeply, you are at the top of ten old stone steps going down an arched passage. They are worn with time, and made of a very special marbled stone. The passage is lit with candles, set onto wrought metal brackets fixed to the walls. The passage is cool and peaceful and I want you now to take a pace onto that top step, number 10. As you do, it glimmers with a warm light. Now when you are ready, take one more slow pace, onto step nine. Count the steps in your head with me. As it too starts to glow, step ones light fades. As you feel the cares and pains of the outside world fall from your shoulders, let them sag, and move onto step eight. Your head and eyes are heavy, but your heart is light, as you step down onto number seven. All you can hear is the music, and all you can see is the lit up steps, as you progress onto number six. From step six to five, and you can now see a door dimly at the bottom of the steps. Onto four, and you can see the door is very old, with large metal hinges and studding between its worn timbers. It doesn't look as if it has been used recently. On to step three, and remember you are safe, and could get back any time you liked by just opening your eyes, but of course you don't want to. Onto step two, you are nearly there. The music is coming from behind the door and you can see the massive key is already in the lock. Quickly onto step one and turn the key. It is stiff but will move. Open the creaking door slowly and go inside.

(2)   You are standing in a small room. It is dimly lit, but warm and perfumed. There is a small pool, with a stool beside it. Why don't you go sit on that stool awhile and gaze into the pool. At first you will just see your own reflection, but as it ripples you can see many other things. I will leave you here now, and will return for you in a little while.........

(3)   Hello again, I hope you enjoyed looking into the pool. Remember all you saw there. I want you now to scoop up some of the water in your hands and drink it. It tastes good

and sparkling. As you swallow it down, feel a warm blue healing light passing down through your body, making you feel fit, young and healthy. You are ready to face the challenges of the outside world once more.

(4)   It is now time to step back up to that world. Do not worry, you can come back here whenever you want to. Open the door and step onto step 1. The door closes behind you. Up to step 2, counting in your head with me. 3, and the candles light the way upwards. 4, and you are feeling strong, confident and refreshed as you return to the surface. 5, and you are half way there, 6 and you can make out the archway at the top of the passage. 7, and you are almost running. 8,you are returning under your own will. One last lingering step on 9 and you are onto the top step 10. Walk out of the passage and back within yourself. When you are ready, open your eyes, stretch and return to the outside world.

When you have returned, write down and if possible discuss what you have seen and heard as soon as possible

PATH No. 2

Shows a different way of creating those initial 10 steps. Another quite basic, but effective path.

(1)　　As you breathe in deeply, you can smell the earthy scent of a wild wood, and hear the wind through the branches of its trees. Now look at that old oak tree in front of you, with its gnarled, weatherbeaten trunk. It is on the edge of a grassy bank, and its old roots have spread out, breaking the surface in places to maintain its long grip on both this world and the one beneath. The roots form ten descending steps, which I want you to climb down with me. They are steep, but you can support yourself on the trunk to your side. You are on the top step, number 10 now and reaching your foot down to number 9, then 8. The outside world is fading away. Step 7, and all you can hear is the distant music and your own heavy breathing. Step 6, and its getting dimmer now, so you move almost by sense of touch. Step 5, and you are getting round to the far side of the trunk from where you started. Step 4, you feel that many have walked this way before, in times past, and you notice an almost hidden, narrow fissure below you in the trunk. Step two brings you nearer to it. A final deep step down and you have arrived below the level of earths surface, ready to enter into that crack in the tree trunk which is just big enough for you to squeeze into.

(2)　　Inside the hollow tree, luminous fungi cast just enough glow to illuminate you way down through the roots to a small cave. Stalactites and stalagmites glitter, and in the centre is a stone pillar. Look at the markings on it and surround it with your arms to know its secrets. I will return for you in a little while.........

(3)　　Hold the stone again, and feel the stored warmth flowing into your body. It is healing all your hurts, and giving you an inner strength. Now when you are ready, walk back to the gap, and squeeze through.

(4)   You are through the gap, and starting back up the steps made of tree root. 10, and you are on your way, 9, and you feel the fresh air on your face. 8, and the way is easier now. 7, and you are rounding the bend. 6, and you can see a glimmer of light ahead. 5, and you are moving as one with great experience in such things. 4, and you are ready to face the real world again. 3 and you are nearly there. 2, and a final heave brings you back up to the surface. When you are ready, open your eyes.

Note that the numbering is reversed on the way back. This was deliberate, and is often done. Some people work better this way.

PATH No. 3

This path shows that you do not always have to set your workings in the mystical past.

(1)   As you relax, you can see an old type of red telephone kiosk in front of you. Step inside, and relax. You are still in the present, but your body is protected from the outside world within its walls. Pick up the receiver, and put your finger in the old metal dial at 0. Push it round to the end stop, and let it slowly return. As it does, the windows steam up, and a spark from your life force is forming just behind your lips. Now dial 9, and see that sparkling ball of energy slip into the mouthpiece. Your body is still safe, but your energy can go anywhere in the world where the telephone system extends. 8, and you can see the copper wires with their multicoloured insulation around you. 7, and you are heading down the cable towards the telephone exchange which is going to send you to anywhere in the world you would like to go. 6, and you are through the exchange, heading outwards, on undersea links, via satellites or whatever. 5, you are feeling good. You are in control. 4, and you are nearly there. 3, travelling at fantastic speeds.

(2)   2, if you want to go on from the first destination, you can do it via any telephone. 1, you have arrived. I'll call you back a bit later......

(3)   OK, time to return your call. Back into the phone line you go, and heading for a very special circuit. There are the usual resistors, capacitors, transistors, coils and microchips, but connected together in a unique new way. They are filtering out the negativity from you, amplifying you and making you stronger. Go round the circuit as many times as you like.

(4)   Its time to return to the room now - you can go directly there, and back into your body. In front of you is a modern telephone keypad. Just by thinking, you can operate the buttons to get you back. Do it with me. * (Either use your

own home telephone number with an STD code to give ten stepped numbers, or make one up.)

*I actually used a telephone keypad that made the musical tones at this point for realism, but this isn't really necessary, and you could just as well reverse the dial sequence used in section (1).

PATH No. 4

You may always prefer to get down the same way, and shamen invariably repeat a successful method so that it becomes easy and 'second nature'. It is up to you personally, and there can be endless, inventive variations on the ten step theme. Just make sure that you take your time on it though, or it will not work whether fancy or simple. This path has got yet another variation on the ten steps.

(1)   Its a hot summers day, and you are alone in the back garden of an old country cottage. The flowers are out and the insects are buzzing about. You want to escape somewhere cooler and quieter. In the corner of the garden is an old well, with a bucket slung beneath its protective roof. The bucket is large enough, and safe enough to hold you, so get into it. By releasing the rope a little at a time,that hangs beside the basket you can gently lower yourself down. Do it in easy stages with me. 10, 9, 8, and the world outside is disappearing a mere disc of light above your head. 7, 6, 5, and the only sounds you can here is the creak of the rope and the water running below. 4, 3, 2 and you are nearly to the bottom. You can see a ledge beside the underground stream that feeds the well. 1, and you step out of the bucket onto it. The bucket will stay where it is for you to return in.

(2)   As you move along the ledge it gets wider, and you find a small boat for you to step into. No need to row, - the current will take you gently along. There are strange markings on the wall, and you realise you are not the first to travel this way. The cavern widens, and there on an island is someone waiting to answer your questions. I will leave you with them a while......

(3)   It is time to leave now, so pay your respects before you go. Wade into the water, and merge with it. You are becoming a fish, and can let the water heal you of all aches and hurts as it sparkles over you. Swim strongly to where the bucket waits.

(4)   As you jump into the bucket, you resume human form. It is time to return to the surface now, so pull on the rope to go up. 10, 9, 8 and you are moving. 7, 6, 5 and you are holding your memories, 4, 3, 2 and the disc of light is dazzling. 1, and you are clambering out, back into the garden, and the real world.

PATH No.5

A simple addition to the build up can be used when a group is working this one. When you get down to the last tenth of candle, snuff it out. Although everyone elses eyes are closed, they still register the glow disappearing (often with a surprised gasp!) thus adding to the realism of the visualisation. If you intend to do this, you obviously need the candle close at hand, plus some matches to relight it for the journey back.

(1)   Before you go down, look once more at the candle, and fix its image in your minds eye. Remember its warm, comforting glow as you close your eyes once more, breathing deeply, and letting every part of your body rest. As you relax and breathe deep, you are looking down a sloping, curving corridor. In your hand you have a candlestick, with a lit candle. It is about 10 inches high, and lights up the narrow, vaulted walls and ceiling. We are going to walk gradually down that sloping, curved corridor together, in ten stages. 10. You will notice that the candle burns down a tenth, and will do this at each stage. 9, the candle still burns brightly. 8, and the world outside is far away. 7, as the candle burns down, your mind is completely absorbed with the music. 6, and the flickering candle lights the old stone walls as you round the bend in the corridor. 5, and the candle is half gone. 4, and you can see an end to the passage. 3, there is a door ahead, closed by a large bolt. 2 and the candle is almost gone. 1 You are at the door, and although the bolt is stiff you can manage to draw it back. As you open the door, the draught blows out what was left of the candle. (Candle snuffed out here).

(2a)   You are in a small room, lit by a single window, set high up the wall. On the wall, at head height, is a wheel. Set your hand to it and spin it. As it spins, you will see a vision. If you want to, you can step through the wheel and into the vision to alter it, but I will leave that to you. I will return in a little while to take you on further.....

(2b)   It is now time to leave the wheel and the room. Look at your arms. They are sprouting feathers. Your nose turns to a beak, and your eyes are suddenly five times better. As you assume the shape of a bird, fly up and out of the window, and into the sky above. Have a good look round.....

(3)　　　You are approaching a fluffy white cloud. Fly right into it. It will make you feel better about yourself, and help you understand the actions of others. Its penetrating and cleaning you from the inside. It feels sensual, and healing. Enjoy it.......

(4)　　　Time to fly down from that cloud now, and back through the window. As you land on the floor below, watch yourself taking back your old form. The stub of the old candle is still in its holder, so light it now. (Relight candle). Open the door and go through it, bolting it behind you. Start back up the sloping corridor with me now. As you progress up, the candle will grow longer and stronger. 10, and it is lighting the way. 9, taking an easy pace upwards. 8, the flame flickering brighter. 7, and you can see the bend. 6 and you are to it. 5, the light still growing, 4 you are getting there. 3, you can see the top of the corridor. 2, almost there, and the candle returns to its original form at 1. You are back, blinking in the light.

PATH No. 6

Not one of our paths this time, but one created by one of our regular group, Dee. She has shown an original approach to 'getting down', and proved that a beginner with a good idea can be just as effective as more experienced pathworking leaders. We'll have to watch her!

(1)   You are in a garden on the face of a large sundial, standing on the number 12. Step slowly from number to number, 11, 10, 9, 8, 7, 6, 5, 4, 3... On 2 the scene changes to a meadow, on 1, a house appears before you.

(2a)   Step from the sundial and follow the short path to the house. The door is open and you may enter. I'll leave you now to explore................

(2b)   It is time to leave the house now, move through the rooms to find the back door. You walk out into the garden and leave through an old wooden gate at the end of the path. The scene changes and you are standing on a hilltop. A short walk will bring you to your guide. He is sitting cross legged on the grass holding a small wooden box. This contains the answer to a question. Ask your question and wait for him to open the box.......

(3)   As you leave your guide you approach a rainbow coloured fountain. Step under the falling spray and bathe in the cool, healing water, washing away all your problems and stress. Let it flow away into the pool under your feet.

(4)   Stepping from the fountain you ascend a staircase by which you will return, counting the steps as you go. 10, 9, 8, 7, slowly becoming aware, 6, 5, 4, 3 awakening, 2, 1. In your own time return to this time, this place.

PATH No. 7

This path incorporates a double getting down section. This is useful if you have problems getting down deep enough, or getting down at all

(1a)   You are in an old theatre. As you enter the seating area you see that you are the only audience. Walk down 10 rows of seats to the best position in the house. 10, 9, 8, 7, 6, 5, 4, 3, 2, 1. Take a seat in the centre of the row and look at the stage.

(1b)   The velvet curtains are closed, but each side of them are a bank of 5 coloured spotlights. As you look at each one in turn, they will light up. 1, 2, 3, 4, 5 you have lit up one side. Now as you start on the other bank you see the curtain slowly rise. 6, 7, 8, 9, 10.

(2a)   The curtains are now fully raised, and the spotlights illuminate a swirl of dry ice that covers the stage. The music swells as a show starts just for your benefit. You can summon whatever artistes you require to give you the show of a lifetime. Enjoy it!..........

(2b)   The performance has finished now, and the curtain descends once more. An usherette beckons you out of your seat with a torch. Follow the usherettes torch. You cannot see her face, but you sense its someone you know and trust. You are being taken through a door at the side of the stage, and down into the dark recess beneath it. Many props and costumes are lying about, left over from years ago. Why not try on a costume and use the props. Your guide will help you stage your own act, and put your make up on..................

(3)   Time to end the performance now. Go through the door at the end to the star dressing room. Look at yourself in the lit up mirror as you wipe the sweat and make up off with a small pad. It smooths the wrinkles and makes you feel good. It is cool and soothing.

(4)   Back out to the auditorium now. Look at the spotlights, and dim them one by one. 10, 9, 8, 7, 6, 5, 4, 3, 2, 1. Now walk backup past the tiers of seats to the lit up exit sign. 10, 9, 8, 7, 6, 5, 4, 3, 2, 1. You are back to the outside world. Let your eyes gradually readjust to the light.

PATH No. 8

If any reader recognises a certain element of this path, yes, I am a fan of C.S. Lewis books too, and have no shame in adapting ideas from anywhere!

(1)   As you sink down to the levels beneath the surface, be aware of an old round stone tower in front of you. It has a sturdy oak door at its base, with 10 locks running down its right hand side. In your hand you find the master key that will open all 10, starting from the top and working downwards. Turn the key in lock number 1. It moves easily, and as the lock releases, so does a part of you. Lock 2, and a little further. Lock 3 and you are nearly a third of the way down. Lock 4 opens, and you are part of the natural rythmn of the place. Lock 5, and you begin to sense that there is something good behind that door. Lock 6, and the top half is loose. Lock 7, and you are speeding down confidently now. Lock 8, you are ready, but must still open Lock 9. You are relaxed and easy as the last one, Lock 10 opens. The door pulls open to reveal a spiralling stone staircase.

(2a)   You begin to climb the stairs, having pulled the door shut behind you. As you climb, you are aware not only of the cold, damp stone walls, but of some footsteps following further behind you. Do not be afraid. The person who is following is more wary of you than you are of them. They have no wish to frighten you in any way, but given the chance may break their shyness by talking. Why not pause and let them catch you up? Turn to face them as they follow you up the staircase. Ask them a question and then listen to what they have to say.......

(2b)   Leave your friend now and move up to the open window. Look out on the rocks below. At ground level they just seem like boulders in the way, but as you look down on them they spell out a solution you have been looking for. Remember it.

(3)   Upwards to the top of the tower now. Its bathed in a shaft of pure light, piercing through the crack in the clouds to illuminate, refresh and invigorate you. Stretch yourself out in it - let it bathe you all over to remove the imperfections of the outside world.

(4)   You can float. No need to use the steps now, just step over the edge of the tower parapet, and feel yourself drift slowly back to earth. 10, 9, 8, 7, 6, 5, 4, 3, 2, 1 and you are gently deposited on the ground outside the bottom of the tower again. When you are ready, open your eyes to the other world again.

PATH No. 9

I am often sparked off on the idea for a path by something quite simple. In this case it was coming up from a tube station in central London to be confronted by a pleasant green square, set amidst the towering buildings. It was such a cool looking oasis amongst the city bustle, that I felt I must revisit it somehow. This was the result.

(1)   As you close your eyes and relax, you can hear a tube train pull away and feel the hot draught of air rush around you. In front of you is a slowly moving escalator, heading upwards to the surface. Before you step onto it, look at the side wall and you will see ten poster boards. Only the details of the bottom one can be seen, and that has a ladies face that is scowling on it. Step onto the escalator, and go past the picture. As you go past frame number 2, the same ladies face appears, but with just a grimace showing now. Frame 3, and her face is a blank. As the escalator moves you further, on frame 4 you find her looking mildly surprised. Frame 5, and she is peering out, actively intrigued. Frame 6 and she has the beginnings of a grin, frame 7 a wide smile. As you pass the eighth frame she is laughing. 9, and she is relaxed and content. On the last frame 10, she is calm, with her eyes closed and a slight smile on her lips. The escalator has delivered you to the top, so step off and walk through the barrier.

(2a)   Across the road from the tube station is a square of green gardens, surrounded by wrought iron railings. Cross the road carefully to it. It is a small oasis amidst the square of tall buildings that surround it. Enter the gate and enjoy it. You can simply sit on a park bench or walk around. There are autumn colours but it is still mild in temperature......

(2b)   It is time to leave the garden now. Go out by the opposite gateway to the one from which you entered. Standing at the kerbside is your dream vehicle - the one you have fantasised about. It is yours for a while to get away to a favourite place. I will meet you there later......

(3)   It is time for you to join me once again. You are entering a large building. Up some steps and through a revolving door. Some friendly white coated attendants are waiting for you, and show you into a room in which there is an impressive, but mysterious looking machine. One of the attendants helps you onto a couch, and switches it on. It buzzes, and from a nozzle, healing, soothing rays wash all over you. This machine is especially tuned to your needs, and makes you feel really good.

(4)   The machine has a dual purpose. If you look at the side,it has a dial, numbered 10 down to 1. As the needle falls from 10 down to 1, the walls of the building and the machine will dissolve, and you will be returned back to here. Count it back with me. 10, 9, 8, 7, 6, 5, 4, 3, 2, 1 and you are back (with?) your new found friends. Open your eyes when you are ready.

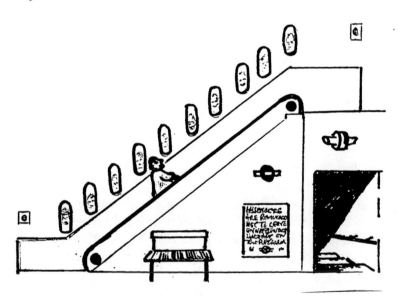

PATH No. 10

(1)   As your eyes adjust to your new world, and your breathing fits to its rythmn, look ahead to the old barn. It seems a bit weathered by age, with patched sides and holes in its thatch. No one has been down this way for years. The large doors are open just wide enough for you to slip through. In the dim half light you can see a ladder leading up to the hayloft. Climb it with me, those 10 rungs, slowly and steadily. 2, 3, 4, 5, 6, 7, 8, 9, 10.

(2a)   Its very dark in the hayloft, except where beams of sunlight penetrate between the thatched roof. There is a slight breeze circulating through as well, and as you watch it pushes some loose straws about on the floor in a circular pattern. Watch the pattern closely, as it may tell you something...........

(2b)   Good! Now that you have had time to look at the pattern, and your eyes have adjusted to the light a bit more, look over towards the darkest corner. What looks like a discarded sack is in fact a small person. They are awake, but shy. They are now aware that you can see them though, and do not want to be recognised. But this is a shapeshifter, and can turn into many other forms! Be still and quiet, and it will change to something you are both comfortable with. When it has reached that stage you can talk to each other......

(3)   Your conversation is at an end. Leave the shapeshifter in peace now. Walk over to where a ray of sunlight is piercing through the thatch. Feel it warm you. Feel it heal you with an inner glow.

(4)   Time to go back down the ladder now with me. 10, 9, 8, 7, 6, 5, 4, 3, 2, 1 and you are down. Walk out of the barn without looking back. Walk 10 paces out(1, 2, 3, 4, 5, 6, 7, 8, 9, 10). When you look back now, you will see the barn has gone, with just grass and earth left in its place.

PATH No. 11

The healing section 3 is a little more subtle in this path, but no less effective in being incorporated into section 1

(1)   Ahead of you as search, is a low, round hut, with mud and wattle walls and a thatched roof, which comes down quite low. An animal skin hangs across its only entrance. Enter the hut with me now - you are quite capable of dealing with everything in it. Pull back the skin and enter, but not too fast. In front of you is a deep pit, and you are standing on the ledge around the outside of it. In the shadows, figures watch silently to see what you do. Rising up from the floor of the pit are ten poles, made from tree trunks. We are going to use them to cross to the other side, counting them down one at a time. As you step onto the first, there is a low murmur of approval around the hut. Step 2 and they hold their breath. Step 3 and you feel them willing you on. 4, and you are growing in confidence. 5, and you are halfway there, but do not rush and spoil it. Take step 6 firmly and deliberately. Step 7 and you can see the figure at your routes ending holding out a helping hand. Steps 8, then 9 and you reach him. He pulls you onto the ledge with him from (3) step 10 and smiles in welcome. It is made obvious by the others you have passed some sort of test,and they are nodding their approval. They pat your back and clasp your hand in welcome to their group.

(2)   The group pull back a skin from the wall revealing another opening, opposite to the doorway. It looks out on a frozen waste. Snow covered mountains drop down to an iceberg strewn fjord. Gaze into that magical place and see the message that is there for you amongst the icy winds that whistle about you.............

(4)   Time to step back into the warm hut now, and time to leave your new found friends. They will always be there for you to visit another time though. Step back across the poles one at a time. 10, 9, 8, 7, 6, 5, 4, 3, 2, 1. You wave your friends

a goodbye and duck back out through the doorway into this other world. Open your eyes when you are ready.

PATH No. 12

Usually, one decides a path and then finds a piece of music suitable to accompany it. This one was the other way round. I obtained a cassette 'Reverence' by Terry Oldfield, who had blended flute and other instruments with the sounds of the sea and whale calls. The path that it inspired is an entertaining and relaxing one, with two section ones to get you really deep.

(1a)   As you drift, you are on the dockside of a Caribbean island port. There are all sorts of craft there, but standing out amongst them is a large, white research submarine. It looks very high tech., and is covered with spotlights and large observation windows. Walk up the gangplank. It is swaying gently with the waves, but is quite safe. You are to take command of this craft, and its computers will pick up your thoughts and transport you where you want to go.The hatch is open in front of you, so step down onto the ladder. You have to go down ten rungs of the ladder, slowly so you do not fall. 1, 2, 3 and you feel the comforting vibrations of the powerful machine beneath you. 4, 5 and the bright daylight outside is now only a disc above your head. Shut it out by pressing the button by your right hand. It will close and seal the hatch above you. 6, 7, 8, and you are nearly to the bridge deck of the submarine. 9, 10 and you are standing on it. All around you are machines and dials and controls, but you do not have to touch them. The computers are locked into your thoughts. Take one last look at the quayside through the windows, and head out to sea on the surface.

(1b)   As you head out to sea, there is a gentle rocking motion from the small waves, but nothing to alarm you. Some porpoises and flying fish are keeping pace with the craft alongside. You are still not too far away from land to lose the seabirds that follow in your wake. Some of them are diving beneath the surface, so why don't you as well, a fathom at a time. We will go down to ten fathoms. Each fathom is six feet, so that is sixty feet. Down 1 fathom, and bubbles swirl around the outside of the windows. 2 fathoms and they clear. 3 fathoms and the suns rays penetrate the surface of the sea in beams, as in a forest. 4 fathoms and it is getting darker, so make sure the spotlights are switched on outside. 5 fathoms, and it is getting cooler too, so raise the heating level. 6 fathoms, and your ears feel a bit funny with the pressure, so swallow hard to clear them. 7 fathoms, and you are in the midst of shoals of fish, attracted by the lights. 8 fathoms and you are nearly down, 9 fathoms you slow down and at 10 you stop, held motionless in the water.

(2a)   Take a good look round. You can also hear, via some external microphones connected up to speakers in front of you the sounds of great whales as they communicate. I will leave you to enjoy the situation for a while...........

(2b)   Whatever you are watching or doing, pause to listen a moment. If you watch closely, you will notice that the fish are all heading in the same direction. Why not follow them? They will lead you to a city, sunken long ago beneath the sea..........................

(3)   You have experienced now all that you can on this dive. You need to return to shore for fresh supplies of fuel and air. Slowly raise the level of the submarine to 10 fathoms. Problems are caused if we go too fast, so continue the ascent with me. 10, 9, 8, 7, 6, 5, 4, 3, 2, 1 and your craft breaks the surface of the sea. The quayside is nearby. Let the craft dock under auto pilot.

(4a)   Now it is time to go back up the ladder. 1 step, 2, 3, 4, 5.

(4b)   Once again, push the button beside you to open the hatch above. Brilliant sunlight and a draught of fresh, tangy salt-sea breeze pour down. Breathe it deep, and feel it doing you good. You had not really noticed how stale and stuffy the air was getting down there. One more big gulp and you are ready to ascend the other rungs of the ladder.

(4c)   6, 7, 8, 9, 10, and you are on deck. Down the gangplank and into your place. Welcome home, Captain!

PATH No. 13

(1)   As you relax and look around, you find yourself in the English countryside on a fine spring morning. There is the twitter of birds and the hum of insects as you breathe in deeply the fresh country air. In front of you is the corner of a field, surrounded by tall hawthorn hedges. There is a gap in the hedge, with a stile. Climb over that stile and walk diagonally across the field to the opposite corner. The ground slopes gently towards it. Here is another stile to climb over, to take you into a second field, full of beautiful wild flowers. Walk steadily across it, still taking deep breaths of the clean country air, and leaving the distant road and houses far behind you. Then its over a third stile into a third field, which has lain fallow many years. It also has a tall hedge surrounding it, so you must once again walk to the opposite corner to find what lays beyond. Another stile to cross, and another field,and you are well away from civilisation and its worries now. Only (2a) one more stile to go. As you climb over it, you see a large round ball shape hovering the next field. Walk right up to it, and you will find it is a balloon basket, waiting to whisk you away. Climb into the wicker basket and release the rope. It is all very safe, and it slowly rises with you into the air....... After a while you find that the balloon is keeping to a steady altitude. Look around you and beneath you as you drift gently on the breeze........

(2b)   The balloon is drifting slowly down now, to some land beside a river. There is only a slight jolt as it lands, and you clamber out. The excitement has made you hot and sticky, so go step into the cooling river. Its water is crystal clear, and you can see small minnows darting about in the shallows. As you wade in the water you are very aware of its currents, and the way the different layers are at different temperatures. As you watch your feet dissolve and merge, followed by your legs and then the rest of your body. You are one with the water, and can flow wherever it flows. Let yourself be taken along with it....................

(3)   You are approaching a shallow sandy part of the river bed now, so slowly think yourself back into your own familiar shape. When you are ready, step out of the water onto the shore. Close by is a glowing golden archway. Step into it, and let it caress your body with its healing rays. If there is someone else you know who needs its powers, visualise them in there with you. It makes every part of you vibrate with a natural healing power....

(4)   Now it is time to step out from the archway and resume your place in the physical world. I will count you back. 10, 9, 8, 7, 6, 5, 4, 3, 2, 1 and you are there.

PATH No. 14

The village festival scene in this produced some strong imagery within our group, and was popular enough for us to want to revisit it on subsequent occasions. Some members became so involved with their alter-egos there that it was suggested it was like a psychic form of the Archers - an everyday story of pathworking folk! Anyway, we hope you both enjoy it and learn from it.

(1)   There are ten steps to take down a woodland path before you reach your destination, so take deep breathes and walk them with me. 1, 2, 3, 4, 5, 6, 7, 8, 9, 10.

(2a)   You are deep within an ancient wood, but on the hillside is a small shelter. Make your way up to it and see what you can find there.....

(2b)   It is time to leave the shelter now, and to follow the path that runs around the side of the hill...Look down and you will see a small village in the valley. It has been left behind from the modern world, and still has old values and ways of doing things. It is self contained, and needs no contact with elsewhere, so leave your usual persona behind to become what you really want to be. There are some friends of yours there, and today is a public holiday for the village festival. They will be very pleased for you to go and join them, so go down the hill to them now and join in their celebrations.......

(3)   It is time to say farewell to your friends now, so thank them for their kindness and say farewell until the next time you can visit them. A guide is tugging at your sleeve to show you the way home up the hill. The guide is very wise, and has many comforting words and great knowledge for you alone to hear, so walk beside them now as they climb the hill with you..........

(4)   It is time to come back now, and the guide is leaving you. The guide can be reached again another time. As I count you back, each number will dim the scene you are leaving

behind until it is completely dark, and you are back in the old familiar room. 10, 9, 8, 7, 6, 5, 4, 3, 2, 1.

PATH No. 15

(1)   As you relax, the sigh of the seas waves breaking on the shore in time with your breathing reaches your ears. Visualise those waves gently rolling in one at a time. As the tide ebbs in, each wave takes you down a level in consciousness. 1, 2, 3 and you feel the breeze on your cheek. 4, 5, 6 and the salty tang of the sea spray is on your lips. 7, 8 and the wind is tousling your hair. 9 the water is lapping round your feet. 10 and there is a rigged sailing ship before you, swept in on the tide and waiting for you to board her before she is left high and dry.

(2a)   Get on board, and she turns from the shore to bear you away. There is no one else on board, but the ship can sail itself quite safely. It is taking a course parallel to the coast, which is to your left. Now the ship turns shorewards, making for a small gap in the rocky cliffs that form the land. As you sail through the gap, they cut the wind down and slow the boat as it passes through the channel between them. There is a gently sloping sandy beach to run up here, and with a soft bump you are beached and able to step ashore without even getting your feet wet. Explore the small village you find here.....

(2b)   A storm is getting up now, and dark clouds are racing across the sky overhead. You are not afraid though, and wish to see its power. Spread out your arms and watch them sprout feathers and turn to wings. See your nose harden and hook into the beak of a fierce hawk. Your eyes can see clearly for miles as you fully transform into a powerful bird. Take off, and fly through the eye of the storm to a point above it, where you can watch its power safely.........

(3)   There is one brightly lit cloud that sends out rays of light from time to time. Try to fly through one of them - it will make you even stronger than you are today........

(2c)   The storm is dying away now, so fly high and wide until you see a shining white hall below. When you see it, fly down through the opening in its roof and land on its floor. Resume your human shape to talk to the halls owner.......

(4)   The hall and its owner is fading, drifting away as wisps of mist. In their place you find yourself back on the seashore. Have you been dreaming? Were you really on a ship, and did you actually fly above the storm as a bird? It seems too real for dreams, so remember what you saw and heard as I bring you back. 10, 9, 8, 7, 6, 5, 4, 3, 2, 1.

PATH No. 16

This path has a two section ones, to get you really deep. The Russian doll motif is not dissimilar to the 'Onion Skin' idea used as an analogy by psychotherapists

(1a)   Relax and laze back, as you stretch out on the grass on top of a small hill. Breathe deeply, and let the atmosphere of this ancient barrow rest your entire body. There is nobody else around but you, and you watch fascinated as an ant struggles to negotiate the blades of grass which to it must seem like a jungle. You follow it with your eyes to a crack in the ground which it disappears down. Look closely, and you will notice that the crack connects up with many others, forming a rough line across the top of the hill. With your hands, push the two sides of the crack apart. There is the top of a pole protruding, and as the earth falls away to the vast hollow cavity below you realise this pole is a crude but safe ladder down to it. Descend the ladder slowly with me to enter this hidden world. 1, 2, 3 steps and pause to get your breathe. 4, 5, 6 and the crack above is now the only source of light. 7, 8, 9 and you are nearly to the bottom. 10, and you feel the firm soil beneath your feet, and the earthy smell of your surroundings.

(2a)   The cavern is dome shaped, and as your eyes adjust to the dimness you see little around you but the symbols on the walls. Take a good look at these, and see if you can find a message in them for you......

(2b)   You have seen and understood all you can for now. It is time to leave. Think yourself into the form of a ladybird, which is a beautiful flame red with black spots, and fly back up through the opening above. As you circle round to get your bearings the crack closes itself up again. You will now know which way to head, and will eventually come upon a fine temple. Fly right down into it........ As you alight on the floor, change back to your human form. In front of you on the altar is a Russian doll that seems strangely familiar. Lift the top doll to reveal a slightly smaller version beneath it. Each time you expose another doll it is like shedding one of your own outer skins. In this very private temple you do not need them, as there is no one else to have to present a 'front' to. Then lift that up to reveal another, and another. Now a fifth, then a sixth. As you do, notice that each successive face is more like your own, but without any worry lines or other signs of stress. Reveal the seventh doll, and realise how artificial those outer skins often are. The nearer one gets to the centre, the inner dolls are finer in detail and untarnished by the world outside. The eighth gives way to the ninth. Careful now, as the last shell is removed. What is inside is a tiny, living, image of yourself, pure and uncorrupted by outside influences. It has no need for deceits. Listen to what it has to say......

(3)   Nearby in the temple is a fine fountain. Collect some of its pure warm water in a cup, and take it to bathe that tiny representative of your innermost self. Do it gently and with love. After that it is up to you whether you return it to the innermost shell, or whether you destroy all of them but one to keep it in. It depends how much you actually need (4) those other sides of yourself..... Leave it back on the altar of life, and prepare to return. 10, 9, 8, 7, 6, 5, 4, 3, 2, 1.

(1)   In your hand you hold ten playing cards - the ace to ten of hearts. This is a game which you play by yourself and always win, so relax and enjoy it. Place the 10 of hearts face down on the ground in front of you, and you will feel a little detached from the outside world. Now lay the 9 face down on top of it, and you are a little further removed. 8, and you know you have a winning hand. 7, and all the everyday cares are gone. 6 , and you are wondering what adventure awaits you. 5, and you catch the distant glimmer of water in moonlight. 4, and you hear it gently lap the shore. 3, and you are super sensitive to every sight and sound. 2, and the vision is becoming clearer. Now lay your Ace to put you in the picture. Leave the pile of cards lying there

(2a)   A small rowing boat is approaching the shore. The ferryman helps you into the boat without saying a word. He has pointed the boat towards a distant island, where you can see the glimmer of a campfire burning. The ferryman will only answer one question, so think carefully before asking him anything. He will return for you later, and he seeks no reward for rowing you........

(2b)   The island is looming up, so get ready to jump ashore. The boatman will return for you when you are ready. It is a clear, crisp night, so head for the warmth of the fire. Look deep into its flames to see the pictures that live there....

(2c)   You are joined by someone else who has a gift for you. Accept it gratefully and enjoy their company.........

(3)   Your visitor is leaving. Turn back to the fire. Its flames are at your command now, and cannot harm you. Step right into them and they will not burn you. They will simply cleanse, refresh and warm you........

(4)   It is time to call the boatman back. Stand up so that you are silhouetted against the firelight and wave. He will

see your signal and come to row you back. While he does, try and identify who he really is..............................Now that you are back on the shore, find the pile of playing cards that you left lying on the ground. Turn over the top card and lay it face up beside the rest of the pack. Now turn over the two, and put it face up on top of the ace. As you do, the scene around you gradually starts to fade. Now the 3, and the 4 and so on. 5, 6, 7 and you are nearly back, 8, 9 and 10. Welcome back!

8. ADVANCED PATHS

Before we start detailing some advanced paths a word of warning! Do not jump the gun and try these too soon. Some of these do not look too different to the simple scenes set in the last chapter, but believe us they are. You need to be used to going down deep to get the most out of these. Some you may never want to try, because they are designed for particular circumstances which you might not encounter. One or two are very specific. They are shown not because you might need them, but they will give you a model to base your own advanced paths on. If you have ploughed through all the preceding chapters first, and worked all the simpler paths (repeating any you failed to work successfully) you should have a good idea by now how to construct your own. This can then be arranged to fit in with your own particular interests and beliefs, and to solve your particular problems. (If you haven't got any problems, we will of course claim it is all due to you following the previous chapters!)

A few of the advanced paths are particularly set for Pagan or Wiccan use. Up until now the paths could conceivably be used by people of any religious beliefs. Many of the paths in this chapter can be followed by anyone, but Pagans, witches etc. are frequent users of these techniques both to assist with astral travelling (i.e. Deliberately attempting out of body experiences) and to gain occult knowledge and insight. This book is not designed to be an introduction to those worlds although both authors are pagans. Please consult the book and contact list at the back if you need further enlightenment. However, if you wish to try some of them without further reading, we advise on those ones where it is shown as appropriate to open a protective circle around yourself first. This must be closed down afterwards as well.

If you have a form of words and ritual from elsewhere, fine. It is even better to devise your own, adapting it from traditional sources, if only to change the words to something you are most comfortable with. You can use the following as a basis if you wish. We have deliberately kept it simple, and not referred to any specific Pagan branch or deities.eg Norse, Celtic, Egyptian, Eastern, Greek, Red Indian etc.

(You will need four candles and holders, plus an athame ritual knife if you have one. If not, use your right index finger to point with. Incense can be from a joss stick or charcoal burner, and a cup of water plus a pinch of salt is also required. You will have to sort out which direction North is first.)

To open circle, first set out the candles to the four cardinal points, North, East, South and West. Consecrate the water by adding salt to it, (traditionally the chalice or cup is stood on a pentacle for this, but if you haven't got one, do not worry.) While you are doing this, put the point of the athame or finger into the cup and say:

"Blessed be, water of the ocean and salt of the earth. Pour blessings on all that you touch, and cleanse this place of all evil. I ask this in the names of (insert own personal deities here or 'the Old Ones')"

Sprinkle the water around in a clockwise circle, starting and finishing in the East. Visualise a glowing circle of light as you do it, and say:

"I consecrate this boundary between this world and all others, with the essence of land and sea", Similarly waft the incense around the circle, clockwise from the East, saying: "I consecrate this boundary between this world and all others, with the essence of fire and air". Facing East again, point and describe the shape of the Air pentagram in the air thus, and say :

East-Air / South-Fire / West-Water / North-Earth & Ice / Spirit Raising pentagrams.

"I call upon the Guardians of the East to give protection over your domain within this circle, that it may stand good" Then move to the South, and make the sign of the pentagram of Fire. Make the same invocation, substituting "South" and "Fire". Then move to the West, and make the sign of the pentagram of Water. Make the same invocation, substituting "West" and "Water". Finally face North and make the sign of the pentagram of Earth and Ice. Make the invocation one final time, substituting "North" and "Earth and Ice". You will notice the pentagrams for raising and banishing are simple to remember if you think of the pentagram starting from the point for which it is named on raising and going back to that

direction on banishing. Not all pagans keep to these directions, but there is no 'right' or 'wrong' way. If it feels right, do it, is the usual rule! Finally say: "In the names of the old Gods and Goddesses I have raised this circle. May they look on me in protection. " Then make the Spirit pentagram. You have now raised your circle.

You may also wish to invoke particular deities special to you at this point. Otherwise, you are now ready to work the path you have chosen within it.

At the end of your pathworking, you might like to give thanks to your Guardians before closing the circle. Close it as follows, working anticlockwise from the East this time.

East-Wind / North-Earth & Ice / West-Water / South-Fire / Spirit Banishing Pentagrams

Facing East, make pentagram of Air banishing and say:

"Great Guardians of the East, Thankyou for your help and protection. Please return freely to your own realm now - Farewell!"

Facing North, make pentagram of Earth and Ice banishing and say "Great Guardians of the North, Thankyou for your help and protection. Please return freely to your own realm now - Farewell!"

Facing West, make pentagram of Wind banishing and say: "Great Guardians of the West, thankyou for your help and protection. Please return freely to your own realm now - Farewell!"

Facing South, make pentagram of Fire banishing and say: "Great Guardians of the South, thankyou for your help and protection. Please return freely to your own realm now - Farewell!"

Face North once more and make Spirit banishing pentagram, saying: "This circle is now closed - we all go in peace." Dispose of remnants of candles, incense, water etc. in running water, or bury in earth. You should not re - use them, thus causing a 'hangover' from one circle to the next.

Some of the more advanced paths require you to go down very deep in your subconscious, so make sure you carry out the steps down properly in the first sections. If needs be, introduce a second sequence of steps to assist you. Many people, (especially those following a shamanistic line) always use the same tried and tested scenario for reaching the required state. We strongly advise you do not use any artificial stimulants such as drugs or alcohol. Apart from being unnecessary, they can often distort what you see, harm your body and produce false results. If you do need extra aid in becoming particularly sensitive for a path working, do not eat for twelve or twenty four hours beforehand. This will make you slightly light headed, to enhance your perception, but can be cured afterwards by pigging out!

PATH No.18

A Working designed for a particular purpose - to relieve a depressed state of mind. It is rather more abstract than most, but used carefully can be very effective. You will notice that the healing element is incorporated into sections 1 and 2, so that the journey can be taken free of outside cares.

(1)   As you relax and clear your mind, you are faced with a succession of large walls, one behind the other. They are tall and wide, like the barriers we put up around ourselves, and block out the light, making it quite dim. Look at the first wall. The stone blocks are large and heavy. They have been compressed by the enormous pressures of the earth, and even now push and squash each other. The weight of the ones at the top press down on those at the bottom, and the sides press and lean in towards the centre.

(2)   Move to the centre of the wall where all the pressures are concentrated, and you will find an iron ring, set into one small stone. Pull it with all your might. As you do, it will assist you by shaking itself free. It doesn't want to be in such a place. As it comes out, the rest of the wall tumbles down in front of you, as it is robbed of its keystone. Walk through the rubble to the second wall. There's a little more light now, and it will get brighter with each wall you destroy. This one is different. Its covered in a sticky, treacly substance, that clings and stretches when you touch it. It is made of lethargy, inaction, sloth and apathy. But it is insubstantial. Push against it and it will collapse. Go on, push it now. It falls and you step over its gooey remains. A little more light gets through. The third wall is more like a nearly invisible screen, or force field. It is made of negativity. It is built up of the negative thoughts of both you and others. Like all forces, it can be cancelled out by an equal and opposing force, so think of one really positive thing. It could be something you have done in the past, or intend to do in the future. As you concentrate, you will see the force fizzle out to a few dull sparks on the ground. Step over them. You can

hardly see the sparks as the sun shines through even brighter. The last wall is the most substantial. It is darker than black, and is made of fears. You must not totally destroy this wall, as it can serve a useful purpose in delaying us from taking unwise actions. Sometimes though, it gets too powerful so we are going to do something about that. On the ground near you is an ordinary household door, with a handle but no lock. It is quite light, so pick it up and lean it against the wall. You will see the hinges fix themselves to the wall. Pull on the handle, and the door opens to reveal a way through the wall of fears. Go through it into the dazzling sunshine land that waits on the other side.

(3)   There are green fields, flowers and streams here. There are old rocks and pleasant buildings. Make yourself at home. Be what you want to be. See what you want to see and hear what you want to hear. Most of all, feel what you want to feel. Make the most of it until I come to take you back.......

(4)   Sorry, but it is time to go back now. Don't worry though - you can come back when ever you want now the barriers are broken down. Walk back through the door of the wall of fear. The wall isn't as high as it used to be. Step over the smouldering ruins of the negativity screen. Jump for joy over the sticky remains of the wall of lethargy - you don't want any of it to cling onto you on the way back. Finally, pick your way through the smashed up rocks of the wall of pressures. You are back in the room now, so open your eyes when you are ready.

PATH No.19

It has always been considered a valuable lesson in mutual understanding to be able to see things from the other persons point of view. This path helps the members of a group do just that! The path also has a rather effective section 1 for those who find difficulty in getting down.

This path requires some simple forward planning, which well repays the effort. Read the complete thing through to yourself first. You may want to ensure that certain members are sat in specific places. Before starting this path, ensure that the group are in a roughly circular formation. Without explaining why, ask them to look at the person on their immediate left, and remember them.

If you are planning to do this path and there is a second pathworker you can let in on the secret, this can be made even more effective. Get them to sit to your immediate left and take over the path reading at the point indicated * "We are changing, we are changing, we are changing etc"* If you decrease the volume of your voice as they increase theirs, gradually overlapping and then being substituted altogether, it seems to the others you actually have changed into the person on your left! Obviously, you need to be close enough together for them to take over this book, and have enough light without there being too much disturbance. Have a mini rehearsal with your co-conspirator beforehand without the rest of the group being present to iron out any misunderstandings. Doing it this way also means that for the second half of the path someone else is controlling, enabling you to go off on an unhindered trip!

(1)   As you drift downwards I want you to see a door with a step down immediately in front of it....when you have it fixed in front of you, move forward, down the step and push the door open. Step through it onto a wide step, which permits you to close the door behind you. Now take another step down, and open the next door in front of you. This second step and door is just like the last, so close the door behind you. We are going to continue like this for a total of ten steps

and doors - step door, step door. We are up to number 3, so step down, open, and close the door. And so on with 4....and 5,...(we are halfway there) and 6,.... and 7.. and 8 (nearly there, but take it steady, you mustn't trip) and 9,.....and at last 10.

(2a)   The last step and doorway has led you into a deep chamber. In the centre is a large fire to warm yourself by, and its flickering flames light the room. By the light of them, as you look round, you can see many other doors leading into it, and in front of each of the doors one of your fellow travellers. Turn to your left, as they all do, so the person in front of you has their back to you. You have your back to the person behind you, and so on, in a circle round the chamber. The person in front of you is the one who was to your left back in the other world above. As you watch them, you see their spirit step out of their body and into the one in front. Now you do the same. It is perfectly safe, and you may return back to yourself whenever you want.

   ****We are changing, we are changing, we are changing, changing, changing, changing.*****

(2b)   But now you can feel what it is to be that other person. To feel their feelings, see through their eyes and move with their bodies. Experience what it is like to be someone else............... O.K., it is time to step backwards into your own body now. Just let go and drift gently back. Remember what you have learnt.

(2c)   You have seen what it is like to be someone else completely. Now how about seeing someone you once was? On the walls, mirrors have appeared. Look and see the face of one of your previous selves, a past life.......

(2d)   Now you have seen all you can see here, look back to the centre of the chamber. The fire has gone out, and between the ashes you can see a light grating. Get the others to help you slide it away. It is the entrance of a short tunnel, which you all drop down into. It is a tall tunnel, and you have no difficulty in walking along it with the others. It leads out onto a small hillside. Below is a quiet village. They know you there, so why not walk down and say hello?.........

(3)   It is time to leave the village now, and someone is tugging at your sleeve to lead you gently away. They lead you through the streets and to a tower that stands on the outskirts. Step inside, and you will see a chalice filled with a liquid form of love. Take some sips from it, but leave some for others who will follow after you......

(4)   It makes you feel drowsy, and the tower starts to fade in front of you. You are returning back to the other world. You have been away too long. As I count down, you will return to the old familiar room. 10, 9, 8, 7, 6, 5, 4, 3, 2, 1.

PATH No.20

Sometimes others can pick up things about us that we cannot find ourselves. This following path can be used to try and achieve this. It uses a very personalised way of getting down, which may especially help some people.

(1)   As you relax, a modern basement room appears before you. Dominating one wall is a large, heavy strongroom door, with a combination lock and a metal plate fixed to it. Engraved into the plate is your name. You are going to open this door, using the combination lock. The combination is your own birth date, in its eight number sequence. Turn the dial slowly. The first two turns are the numbers for the date of the month of your birthday. Use a nought in front of it if it is a single number, turning the tumbler dial to the pointer arrow mark at the top...Now that you have done that, the next two numbers are for the month of your birth, with a nought in front if it is one of the first nine months. Good, the mechanism of the lock is half open now, and you are wondering what is inside I expect, so complete the combination with the full year of your birth. Do it slowly so that you don't make a mistake......

(2a)   Now you can swing the door open, to reveal a comfortable room, with an old leather armchair and a T.V. set. Beneath the t.v. is a video machine. On a shelf, is three sets of videos, one set with yellow covers, one in green and the other in black. The videos are of your past memories - like living photograph albums or scrap books. The black ones are (3) all the things you would rather forget, so take the pile of them and throw them in the bin in the corner. You do not need them any more. Then select one of the yellow ones and put it in the machine to play. switch the video and t.v. on, and sit back in the armchair to watch and enjoy some of the things that you have done or seen in this life..............

(2b)   The yellow video is finishing now, so go and select one of the green ones. This film is also of things you have enjoyed in the past, but in one of your previous lives. Put the yellow video back in its box, and get the green one ready. Take it and put it on the machine, and watch this too.......

(2c)   The green video is also finishing now. Take it out of the machine and put it back in its case. You could watch something different now if you wished. Your set is connected to a central archive system. Switch it to channel 11, and you may see one of their past lives films. It is the past life of another member of the group......

(4)   You have seen all you can for today now. Switch the machines off, and walk back out of the strongroom door. Push it shut, and then lock it by turning the dial ten times with me. When you have done that, you will be back in your old familiar surroundings. Turn the dial once, twice, three times, and remember all you saw. 4, 5, 6 and the door is closed fast. 7, 8, 9, just to make sure, and 10, you are back.

PATH No. 21

There are many schools of thought regarding past life regression, and we do not intend to be drawn into the debate here. What we do state is that we believe the following to be a simple, cheap and effective way of trying to achieve it. We do suggest that you first read some books on the subject, and that you learn never to 'lead' the subject into characters, events or areas. The subject must be brutally honest with themself, and acknowledge where previously viewed books and films has had an influence on their subconscious state. The technique of opening the eye leads the subject down to deeper levels, and it is surprising how hard it is to open the eye a third time even if you try hard. To be effective the 'going down' stage 1 must be done slowly and thoroughly.

You will need to make sure a single candle is placed centrally for the subject(s) to see. It is not advisable to try and do this solo, or for the pathworking leader to 'join in'. A constant watch should be kept for any signs of distress, and the subject(s) brought back swiftly if needs be.

(1a)   Relax and breathe deeply, with your eyes closed. Your toes are numb already, and that same restful stillness is to creep upwards through your body. Your legs are heavy, your thighs are heavy. A great peace fills your stomach and chest. Your arms and hands are limp, and your neck muscles relax, letting your head rest where it lays, like a heavy rock. Your eyelids are leaden, and do not want to open.

You are at the top of some flights of stairs, and are going to go down them one at a time with me. First one step. Then 2, 3, 4, 5, 6, 7, 8, 9, 10. You have reached the bottom of the flight of stairs. Now wait until I say when, but in a moment I want you to half open your eyes in a slit just big enough to see the candle flame, and then shut them tight again. Ready? Then do it now.....Good. Your eyes are now more tightly shut than before, but do not screw them up.

(1b)   You are at a lower state of consciousness than before as well, and we are going to lower that even further by going down another flight of stairs, one at a time. With each step you will go down deeper. 1, 2, 3, 4, 5, 6, 7, 8, 9, 10. We are going in a moment to try and glimpse the candle once more, but some might not manage it, as by now your lids will be so very heavy. If you do not manage it, don't worry. Try it now, opening them just a slit and closing them again quickly. OK, you are now very deep, but need to be deeper down in yourself than you have ever been before.

(1c)   There is one final flight of stairs to face, so step down them one at a time with me keeping you safe, and you still in total control of yourself. 1, 2, 3, 4, 5, 6, 7, 8, 9, 10. This time, you are deeper than you might have thought possible, and if you tried, you would find it extremely difficult to open your eyes again...

(2)   You are in a library of many books, all old and bound in rich leather with golden clasps and locks. One book is unlocked though, and is laid on an ornate lectern. It is the book of your past lives, and you may go over and look at it now. If there is anything you prefer not to see, simply turn the page...............

(3)   It is now time to close the book. Remember all that you have seen and walk over to where two pillars form a bright gateway. No one can change the past, but here you can be healed of its effects, and reconciled to the way it shaped your future. The light pouring from the gateway onto you will help you to be mentally and physically stronger......

(4a)   It is time to start back up the steps again, on the bottom flight. Go up them with me. 10, 9, 8, 7, 6, 5, 4, 3, 2, 1 and you are at the landing. You will be able to open your eyes fully. Do that and then close them again.

(4b)   You are on your way back. Up the middle flight of stairs now, but do not rush. 10, 9, 8, 7, 6, 5, 4, 3, 2, 1. Open your eyes fully once more and then close them again.

(4c)   Now start back up the last flight. You are feeling confident and fit to face the world again. 10, 9, 8, 7, 6, 5, 4, 3, 2, 1 and you are fully back. This time when you open your eyes, keep them open!

Some people thoroughly enjoy this past regression path, whilst others find it slightly scary. For those reasons alone it is advisable not to repeat it too often within a group, and then only with the people who appreciate it. There is a danger in concentrating on any one type of path too much within a group of mixed interests and abilities.

A variation you can make to this path is to make the book a book of the near or distant future, and to give the participant the ability to change just one thing within it.

PATH No. 22

You may like to cast a circle for this - instructions at the beginning of the chapter. We have included the following path, with the purpose of showing that there are completely different ways of going travelling than the system previously shown. It is known as the Christos Experiment, and there are various forms of it. The variation which we are going to show comes from two of our Ipswich Pathworking Group members, Polly and Dan. It is not for the faint hearted, and one must really trust the others who assist you. It can only be done for one person at a time, so might suit a night when there are just four of you meeting. One will be the subject, one the scribe, writing down or tape recording what happens. This is necessary, as the subject may only have hazy recollections when they return. The other two assist in the following way. The subject lays with their back to the floor, with head and feet on cushions. Their shoes and socks need to be removed also. It is helpful for the room to be dim, but no music is used. One assistant gently massages the feet. It may tickle at first, but this soon passes. The other assistant, who is in control, massages the forehead of the subject at the 'third eye' position with one finger only, and encourages them to close their eyes and breathe deeply and slowly. They also instruct the subject that they must always respond to questions, even if it only to refuse an answer. The controller must maintain this conversation, however awkward, without making judgements or suggestions. ie. "What colour is it?" rather than "Is it red?" and "Where would you like to go?" rather than "Wouldn't you like to go to America?"

When the subject is breathing deeply, and is in a relaxed state, they are told that they are still in total control of their body. They are told to think about extending their legs by six inches, and given time to visualise this, and report when it is done. Then the instruction is given to gradually to retract them again. After a brief pause, they are told to do the same thing with their head. Once again, they must report on progress and on successful visualisation be told to retract it again. All the time, the massaging of the head and feet continues, so it is as well for the assistants to find a comfortable position! The subject is further encouraged and reassured of their control. Now the instruction is given for them to leave their body safely behind in the hands of their trusted friends. They are capable of it. No great tension is needed, just allow it to happen! When it does happen, only float as far as the ceiling, and look down and tell what you can see. Now rise through it, right the way through to just above the rooftop. Make careful observations (aloud) of how it looks from up there, and find things you can use as aerial landmarks. Now you can hurtle off anywhere you like to in the world...at any time period. What is it like? Is it hot or cold? What are you wearing? Are there any people about? Can they see you? What are their names? Are you happy or sad? Do you want to go on somewhere else? OK then, travel wherever you want to. When the assistant has judged that enough has been experienced for one session, the subject is encouraged to return, looking out for the familiar landmarks. Get them to look down into the room once more, and say what they can see. They must then be told to return to their body, and when they report they are comfortable, the massage can stop and the analysis begin!

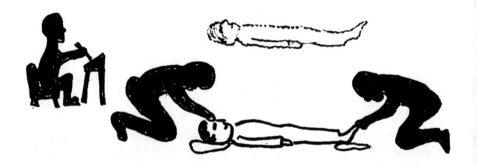

PATH No. 23

This has some special features. One is a way of going down a deeper stage which doesn't involve physically going down. It is a maze, on the level, and you can ignore or heed the advice proffered, thus taking a definite control in your direction.

The second, more important feature is the setting up of a sanctuary. This can be returned to again and again in subsequent pathworkings to alter, expand, modify or to simply enjoy. It can be made so real and personal, that it can be instantly recalled during the stresses of every day life, and can provide an ideal place in which to meditate, learn or do magic in.

The third special feature is getting the group to perform a physical action to effect a change on the spiritual level. This means that you must instruct them to go down initially with their palms closed together, as if in prayer.

> (1a)   As you relax, with your palms closed together, and your breathing deep and even, you see before you a tall hedge, with an opening in it. The hedge is thick, and forms a maze. Its sides tower around you, dark green and thorny, but there is a way through. It involves you in making ten correct turns. I can start you off with the first five directions, but you must decide on the second five, to get you to the fountain you can hear splashing down at the centre. Step through the entrance, and turn immediately to your right. Then take the second turning on your left.....walk along a short way now, ignoring the side turnings, until you get to a T-junction. Turn right at this, making this your third turning. You are in the midst of the maze now, and the curve of the paths confuse which direction you are heading. Trust me though, and take the next turning on your left, which doubles back the way you came from. Walk along it, counting the turnings off to your right. When you reach the fifth one, take it. You can hear the fountain close by now, but this is where I must leave you to finish the maze. You might encounter others, who can offer advice. It is up to you whether you chose to take it though.

When you eventually (2a) reach the fountain, stop and listen to its music and (3a) message, and reward yourself with a refreshing drink. See you there later......

(2b)   Hello again. I am glad to see you made it. It is time to move on now, and to get out of the maze is easy. Look behind the fountain, and you will see it feeds a small stream. Follow that stream out of the maze....... As you leave the maze, the stream widens to a river, fed by some underground springs. Wade into the stream, and submerge yourself in it. You have no difficulty breathing, and as you look at yourself you are changing into a beautiful silvery fish. Swim with the flow of the river. Feel its currents as you course between its twisting banks. You can sense a waterfall ahead, but are not afraid. It is well within your capabilities to leap down it. Go with the flow, as the white water bubbles and froths around you. You have splashed down into a pool. Make for the edge, and as you do, change back to human form. Climb out up the bank, and look back to the hissing torrent you have just leapt. There are some steps cut into the rock at its side, so climb up them now, being careful not to slip on the damp mossy patches. As you walk up the steps, keep an eye on the side of the waterfall. At a place where one of the steps extends into a ledge, move slowly towards it. Don't worry about the spray, you will soon dry off afterwards. The water acts as a curtain across this ledge, but behind it is a hollow. Step quickly through it, and work your way slowly along the edge. The light filters through the wall of water with a greenish hue, illuminating a grotto hidden behind the waterfall. Step into the grotto, and examine what you find there.......

(2c)   OK, it is time to leave the grotto now. Work your way back along the ledge and through the wall of water. Now retrace your steps down to the pool again. Continue to walk round its edge. You can see bulrushes, and flowers, and tiny fish darting about in the shallows. You can also see a small island. Leading to it are the most enormous lily pads you have ever seen - strong enough to take the weight of several

70

(1b) people! There are ten pads, so step across them with me. 1, 2, 3, 4, 5, 6, 7, 8, 9, 10 and you are ashore on the island. Walk towards the clump of trees. Between them you can see a ramshackle old hut, badly in need of repair. Walk towards it, but stop about 25 yards away. Look down at your clasped hands, and look at the hut. Continue to glance between the two. Now keeping the bottom edges of your hands together (the little finger edges), very slowly open your palms up away from each other, as if they were hinged. Thumbs first, and then the index fingers and so on. As you do, the ramshackle huts room also opens up, and reveals a most beautiful building, growing up from inside. As you move your hands completely apart, it grows upwards and outwards. You can decide what shape, colour and form it will take. It is to be your private sanctuary. Take time to change the outside to your liking. Then move inside and do the same there. However you want the rooms to be, and whatever way you want them decorated, it will be so. Whatever you want to be inside them will appear. Construct the place well- you may often want to revisit it. I will leave you to get on....

(3b)   You must soon leave your sanctuary, but before you do I want to show you one room you have probably missed. Place your palm on the wall in front of you, and it will open up. There is a large domed room beyond, and the dome is made of multicoloured glass, that floods the room with wonderful healing light patterns. Wander around and bathe in these different patterns. Each one has a specific healing purpose. Some remove aches and pains, some sadness and anger. Others get rid of negativity, and replace it with a healthy vigour. Find which ones you need and use them................

(4)   Regrettable though it is, you must leave now. Go back out the way you came in, and stop again when you are about 25 yards away. Turn towards the building, and slowly fold your hands together again, reversing the earlier magic. You will see the building shrink back into its old disreputable form. It is disguised to all but you, and you may bring it back

to you at any time by simply using your hands in the way shown. Now step back across the lily pads. 10, 9, 8, 7, 6, 5, 4, 3, 2, 1. The area around you is shimmering, and fades to reveal you back in the old familiar room once more. When you are ready, open your eyes - but be careful what you do with your hands!

PATH No. 24

Of course, it is possible to pathwork without music. How about trying some poetry? You could chose any piece that strongly evokes a place, and use it to put you into the picture. I enjoy walking in woods, so I can use this following poem that I wrote myself to relive a favourite one, even when I cannot physically get there. When doing one of these, you obviously have to have your eyes open to read, so it is better if you can pre-record the poem onto a tape, and use it as you would a music cassette. Take yourself and any others present down in any of the ways shown that will fit in with the general feel of the poem, and then play the tape. Leave a space for everyone to explore on further, and then either bring them back up or take them on further with elements of another pathworking.

WAYLAND WOOD IN JANUARY...Pete Jennings

Swinging my denim clad leg over the stile,
And hobbling humpty heeled over a muddy path,
An inner voice led me to Wayland Wood.
Way - Land, the very name Norse for sacred grove.
My breaths form their dragon ship figureheads
In the damp January air.

Fungi shelves bracketed on the sides of tree stumps
Proving in death there is also life.
Lichens, mosses, dead leaf litter
And bright berries on a bare bough.
How I prefer your russet colours
To the stark green spread of summer.

Latticed piles of wood are overwhelmed
By the wildness that once hid the Babes in the Wood
And the wolf that guarded Saint Edmunds head.
The wood spirit forgives the men who coppice for gain,
Yet restore open space for Woodcock And Large Skipper to flit.

Thralls sons need for broom handles,
Hurdles and thatching pegs
Allows the Bluebell, Wood Anenome and Early Purple Orchid
A place amongst the Hazel, Oak and Bird Cherry Trees.
Brisk January's bite puts keen edges to the hazel wands
That stain my hand and promise Spring.

PATH Nos. 25 - 28

This particular pathworking exercise will introduce you to the four elements of Earth, Air, Fire and Water. These form the basis of all material aspects of the world in which we exist. They should not be undertaken lightly, but with a degree of caution, especially if the pathworker or participant has an inherent fear of fire, water or even flying. Again it is worthwhile taking note of the necessary precautions stated earlier in this book with regards to signs of distress. However, should you feel confident to undertake this particular exercise, then rest assured that the experience of the four elements will leave you feeling full of wonder, and there will be a general enhancement of your vision of the physical world.

EARTH

(1)   As you relax, and breathe deeply, take yourself down in ten steps, to that level of special awareness in whatever way you find most effective. 10, 9, 8, 7, 6, 5, 4, 3, 2, 1.

(2)   Imagine walking down a woodland path with trees on either side. There are rich woody smells and filtered sunlight. You arrive at a grove circled by grand old trees reaching up to the clear, blue sky. Imagine standing naked in the centre of the grove. Your naked feet begin to sink slowly into the earth until ankle deep. Feel the life force permeating outwards like roots into the earth, and in turn draining life energy from the earth back into your body. Stretch out arms to form branches, fingers to form twigs. Leaves sprout from buds on your fingertips, and your hair becomes vines of ivy. Your flesh becomes wooden, but vibrant with the flowing spirit force of the earth. Allow the woodland creatures and birds to inhabit you, become one with the Earth. The (3) sensation of power should manifest itself as a flow up and down the body, taking from and returning to the earth.......

(4)   To end the visualisation, allow the body to return to its natural form in reverse order, but it is suggested that the transformation be performed slowly until one becomes 'disconnected' from the earth after withdrawing the roots back into the body. Return along the woodland path. You may

now either bring yourself back up the ten steps, or move on to the next element.

FIRE

Before undertaking this particular working it should be noted that Fire is perhaps one of the most powerful and uncontrollable energies in the natural world, and so I wish to propose a few cautionary warnings prior to commencing. The main purpose of this working is to produce energy within the mind and body, and should only be undertaken if you feel that you are able to maintain total control of group or yourself. I can assure you though that this particular working will imbue you with a sense of wonder if you are successful.

(1)   If you are starting afresh, as opposed to continuing on from Earth, relax in the normal way. Then, whether you are continuing or starting afresh, breathe from the tummy rather than the chest, as this will be your physical focal point.

(2)   In your mind visualise a rose in tight bud, and as you breathe the rose begins to open very, very slowly. It is a deep red rose, and with every breath it comes fully into bloom, beautiful and rich red. Within its centre a faint spark of light begins to glow - it becomes brighter and brighter and brighter, spreading out to the petals until the whole rose is glowing with radiant light. With a sudden burst the rose is a roaring flame contained within the shape of the rose. At this point the mind becomes one with the flame, a rushing sensation or deep vibration may be sensed. There is no heat, just pure energy combined with the beauty of the rose. It is important to keep the Fire element contained within the shape of the rose. This is to prevent energy becoming dispersed and forming random paths.

(3)   In order to close down, imagine the scene in reverse order - the fire returning from the mind back to the rose and consequently back to its centre via the petals to the original spark. The rose must be tightly closed to ensure the element is confined.

(4)   Should either mental or physical energy be required during any conscious activity eg. sport, exams or job interviews, then just visualise the rose - believe me, it works! You may now either bring yourself back up the ten steps, or move on to the next element.

WATER

(1)   If not already down, see Earth part (1)

(2)   Imagine you are sitting next to a sparkling brook on a hot summers day. You are alone, and the bright sun is reflecting in the waters surface, making it welcoming to your hot body. The sound of the babbling water invites you to join it.

(3)   Standing up you remove your garments and step into the stream. It is ankle deep, and its coolness and movement ebb away your fears and worries. Slowly, very slowly, you begin to melt into the water. You begin to lose all conscious thought becoming one with the Water. You flow with it, becoming dispersed, diluted. Fish swim within you, and you pass within them as their life provider. The stream becomes a river, eroding the earth that contains it; the river becomes an ocean. Feel yourself crashing upon a rocky shore, feel your inherent power carving the coastline. Feel the mass and depth of your element.

(4)   To return, retrace your journey back to the river, the stream and brook, and re-emerge feeling refreshed and clean. You may now either bring yourself back up the ten steps, or move on to the next element.

AIR

This is the final element and one which with ability may allow you to combine all four, as without Air, life would not exist at all!

(1)   If not already down, see Earth part (1)

(2)   Imagine you are standing on a cliff top or hill, and a gentle breeze begins to blow, ruffling your hair and clothes. Face the breeze and raise you arms. The breeze becomes a gentle wind, but grows stronger and stronger until it is a howling gale. Clouds gather in the sky, changing from white to grey to black. A storm is forming around you and you are controlling it. At your chosen time create thunder, and at the same time bring down a lightning bolt which will pass through your body, shattering it with its power and allowing you to become formless. Join the air and fly free - visit remote lands and scenes of your desire. Pass through forests and skim mountain tops. Become a snow storm or whatever you chose. There are no boundaries in this working. (4) To return, begin a deep breathing exercise and reform your physical self on the cliff top. Allow the clouds to return to white and the wind to become a breeze, until all is still once more.

(1)   You are in a dusty desert setting, with the sun only recently risen, so it is not yet more than pleasantly warm. When in these Eastern places, one should not rush about and expend too much energy, so relax and adjust to the local pace of life. Relax deeply as you watch the ox powering the artesian well before you. It is an old, ramshackle affair, and the ox must walk round in a clockwise circle, attached to a shaft that runs to work the well in the centre of the circle. Sometimes he pauses, to be urged on by a small boy with a stick. As he continues, just concentrate on the pattern he makes with his hooves in the dust. Each time he completes a circle, you will become more and more part of the landscape there, and less of it here. Watch it make one circle, 2, 3, 4 and 5 circles. If you look down at yourself, you have already adopted the flowing native robes. Now a sixth circle, 7, 8, 9, and a final tenth and you are completely there.

(2a)   Stand up and turn around. There is an old Arab walled city, with its huge gates wide open. Not too many people are moving about yet, but there is a dishevelled looking blind beggar, sat on the ground leaning against one of the massive gateposts. Walk up to him. You will see in his lap a small sand tray, in which he writes with his finger. See if you can get the meaning from what he writes for you there.....

(2b)   In your pocket you will find a few small coins. Drop them into his hand, and walk through the gateway. The merchants are setting out their goods outside the shops, and small children are playing a game of tag between the row of tethered camels. Carry on past them, and head down the narrow alley you see to the right. At the end, in contrast to the other dark and seedy buildings is a shining white one. Its fantastically shaped door is covered with highly decorative filigree work, and pushes open to your touch.

(3)   Inside are graceful columns and a marble mosaic floor. On an ornate side table you will find a bowl of rose

water, to wipe away the sweat and grime of the heat. A crisp white towel is beside it, and a goblet with a delicious iced drink to refresh you. Help yourself to something from the tray of sweetmeats as well. Then climb the stairs to the landing.

(2c)   On one wall is a pair of double doors, the golden handles of which are tied together with a piece of white cord. The knot of this cord is sealed in wax. You are entitled to enter here, so look amongst the folds of your clothes for a small scimitar shaped knife, and cut the cord. As you push open the doors, their golden hinges creak with age and disuse. In the centre of the room is a short marble pillar, and on that a large book. This is the book of just one of the futures that is possible for you. There are many others in existence, but this one has been made available to you to see what you might do with it. You are only allowed to change one single factor, so act wisely, and you may only examine one particular period. The near future is at the front of the book, the distant near the back, so chose carefully at which place you decide to open it.........

(4)   It is time to close the book now, and return. Out of the window you see the ox still turning his wheel. As he turns it ten times, so you will return. 10, 9, 8, 7, 6, 5, 4, 3, 2, 1.

PATH No. 30

The rescuing of 'lost souls' can be interpreted in many ways. It can be a shamanic ritual, but not necessarily so, as straight Wiccan methods are also often applied. It can be compared to Christians praying for sinners and trying to 'save' them, but most people who carry this work out would shy away from the idea. The victims to be 'saved' could be those who are sick in some way (mentally or physically) or could be someone thought to be under evil influence of some description, whether that be of some spiritual entity or a human 'black' magician. In some cases it could be the lost souls of those suddenly killed in a disaster, who need help in coming to terms with their situation and help in progressing upwards on their spiritual path. The shaman makes little differentiation in many cases anyway, and regards illness as the outward sign of some evil internal influence.

There is some argument as to whether the victim should be made aware of the efforts to save them, and whether they should be present. You will have to be guided by your own conscience and intuition, but if practical, one would think that the co-operation of the victim would be useful so long as they were aware of the problem and willing to do something about it. This leads us onto the ethical question of whether you should 'help' anyone who has not asked for it? The problem could be there for a specific purpose, to help that person to learn a lesson or grow spiritually. Some people seem impossible to help anyway, and maybe this could be the reason.

Some methods involve the worker taking the problems temporarily onto themselves, whilst others rely on using counter measures such as invoking opposite forces. Whichever way you look at it, this is serious work that needs to be undertaken with the right preparations and protection. You may like to cast a circle, as shown at start of chapter. Preparations should include a self purification and a thorough understanding of the problems likely to be encountered and how to deal with them. One also needs to be mentally agile and sure of your own beliefs, which are certain at some stage to get tested. You can of course structure the entire working around your own set of beliefs and this can be seen in Path No. 31. (For instance, one could travel over Ymirs Eyebrow Mountains from Midguard to Lyjaeberd, the Hill of Healing to appeal to Menglads/Friggas attendant Eira for help in healing someone. One would have to avoid the giants of Jontunheim, and answer to Fjolsvids questioning). There are equivalents of this process within most religious / mythological systems, using different names and jargon of course.

We appreciate that the preceding paragraphs ask almost as many questions as it answers, but at least it gives some idea of the breadth of the problems involved. Do think carefully before you try to do this sort of thing. The good thing is you can often 'feel' or even see the results afterwards, and good deeds often bring their own internal spiritual rewards.

First, one needs to 'link-in' with the person to be helped, by whatever means available. If they are physically with you, great, but if not, is it possible to hold one of their possessions or focus on a photograph?

Next, one needs to call on the help of whatever Higher Forces you personally acknowledge. Let them work through you, and do not be afraid to invoke their name if you are in difficulties. Know your enemy, and in preparing, try to find out whether that enemy has a specific dislike that you can use against it. Hold any useful symbol or rune firmly in your head so that you can project it if confronted. When you have prepared all you can, be confident in yourself. Everyone has the ability to heal - it is not an exclusive gift to the favoured few. All you have to do is allow it to happen!

(1)   Now that you are ready and prepared, take yourself down the usual ten steps in whichever way suits you best.

(2a)   You stand on the edge of a deep, dark, pit. You have a golden cord around your waist that is totally unbreakable, and it is attached via an enormous metal ring to a huge rock, that overshadows the landscape. If you move away from the rock, you find that the cord expands and contracts with the distance like elastic, keeping you safely anchored to the surface. When you are ready, walk backwards towards the pit, holding on to the cord in front of your chest like an abseiling mountaineer. Gently lower yourself over the side, and begin to descend. As you do, the circle of daylight above your head diminishes, but never completely disappears.........

(2b)   Eventually your feet will touch the bottom floor of the pit. Do not he afraid of anything you see there, and do not be diverted from your purpose for being here. Find the one you seek and reach out a hand to them. Banish any who stand in your way by an invocation of the names of the Higher Forces, or by projecting a visualised symbol or rune planned earlier. Do not be fooled by imposters offering false images, promises or advice.

(3a)   Reach out your hand for the one you seek and in doing so transmit a vital spark of life and health to them. You have plenty to spare...................

(3b)   When you have a firm grip on them, look upwards to the sunlight, and let yourself be attracted by it. Let you and your passenger be pulled up towards it, leaving the pit and its darkness behind you.

(4a)   When you have reached the surface, walk back to the shelter of the massive rock to which you are attached. Thank those who have given you help, and then turn to face the mouth of the pit once more. It is already diminished, but visualise it closing over completely, and collapsing within itself.

(4b)   Finally, take yourself back up those ten steps, and if necessary contact those who asked for help to let them know of your success.

PATH No. 31

We now look at pathworking on the Tree of Life. This will provide you with an infinite number of paths to work, lessons to learn and tasks to achieve. Many religions have the allegorical motif of the 'Tree of Life'. It appears in various guises, but generally epitomises the upward struggle to various levels of consciousness or enlightenment, together with a form of map to the spiritual world. There are numerous examples from the East to be found in various cabbalistic books. I however wanted to pathwork within the Northern tradition, so assembled information from various sources to construct the Yggdrasill World Ash in picture form. Some of the sources conflict, so there is no one definitive version within Norse mythology. I actually did it on my home computer, so I can constantly update and amend this Norse 'Pilgrims Progress' as my researches progress.

You could do the same thing for your own beliefs, and it doesn't have to be as elaborate as mine. I would recommend creating it in a form which can be amended though. I have shown my own model on the following pages as an example. The Norse mythology is contradictory, complicated and too vast to cover in this book. I have shown the main deities with their relationships and characteristics for guidance, but suggest some thorough reading if you are to use this example, some of which is shown in the bibliography.

The Tree as you see it is fed by its three roots, which go down to the three levels of the nine worlds. The Norns and wells help to nurture it, but it is under attack by the Nidhogg dragon, serpents and stags. So the World Ash becomes an ecological balancing act, with the forces of good combating those of its survival. From this tree Yggdrasill (meaning Odins Steed) Odin hung for nine days and nights over the Abyss Ginnungagap, wounded by his own spear Gungnir, to gain the knowledge of the runes. (There is obviously a marked similarity with the Christian crucifixion story there).

It follows that if Yggdrasill is Odins Steed, he and the deities of which he is the Allfather of, must work with their followers to ensure the stability of their homes and his throne, which are sheltered by it. If you take the premise that all the deities, giants, dwarfs and elves characters are projections of various aspects of human behaviour, then you can see a pathworking can be used to explore yourself, as well as some mysterious mythological world. It can be used to define or redefine your relationships with both the spiritual and physical world. It can be used to communicate with the spiritual world to achieve healing or divination, and rescuing lost souls.

This is all a very personal process, so it is quite likely that you may want to do this pathworking solo. However, if there are others that you are closely in tune with mentally and emotionally, it is possible to work in a small group.

You may like to cast a circle, as shown at start of chapter

Decide where you want to go, and what you want to achieve first. Make sure you can remember the names, runes, spells etc. that you may need for there. Make sure you have a clear picture in your mind of the route, and then take yourself down those ten steps whichever way you find most effective. You can usually 'think' yourself to a starting place, but if there are obstacles in the way after that, you need to traverse these as they come up. They are obviously there for a reason, and should not be ignored. By all means use incense, candles and suitable music if this helps in the process. If working alone, make sure you have a way to return, as detailed in Chapter 6. Good luck! Further information and charts for the Yggdrasill working follow:

The Norse Deities - Aesir unless annotated V for Vanir.

No pseudonyms used - gender not always constant. Names in small type in first three columns indicate non-deity ie. Giant, human or dwarf. Att. = attendant.

Name	sex	Married to/ lover (1) of	Children	The God of
AEGIR	m	RAN	9 WAVES f	Sea
ALI	m			Marksman known as Vali.
ANNAR	m	NOTT	ERDA f	
AUD	m			
BALDER	m	NANNA	FORSETI m	Purity-Killed by Loki & Hod
BRAGI	m	IDUN		Arts - runes on tongue.
BIL	f			Weaving
DAG	m			Day
DELLINGER	m	NOTT	DAG m	Dawn. (3rd husband)
EIRA	f			Medicine. Att. of Frigga
ERDA	f			
FJORGYN	f		ODIN / THOR m	Earth
FORSETI	m			Justice & Truth
FREY (V)	m	Freygerda	Frodi m	Fertility. Lived with Aesir as hostage.
FREYJA(V)	f	OF	GERSEMI f	Sex, war & death.
		ODIN 1	HNOSS f	Confused with Frigga.
		Ottar 1		Reputed to have many
		Alfrigg 1		other lovers. Last 4
		Dvalin 1		are dwarfs who made
		Berling 1		her Necklace of Brisings.
		Grerr 1		Leads the Valkyries
FRIGGA	f	ODIN	BALDER m	Fertility, housewives.
		Ve & Vili 1	HODER m	Confused with Freyja.
		ULL 1	HERMOD m	Is Menglad in Jontunheim.
FULLA	f			Full haired. Att Frigga
GEFION	f			Virgins. Att of Frigga
GEFJON	f	King of Sweden		The Plough, unmarried women. Att of Frigga.
GERSEMI	f			
GNA	f			Frigga attendant/aide
HEIMDALL	m	Many lovers		Guardian of Bifrost & founder of three races.
HEL	f	ULL 1		Guardian of Hel.
HELGI	m	GUDRUN		
HERMOD	m			Odins messenger son.
HLER	m			An early sea god
HLIN	f			Consolation. AH Frigga
HNOSS	f			D of Freyja & Of.
HODER	m			Blind. Killed Balder.

Name	Sex	Spouse/Partner	Children	Description
HOENIR	m			Early god gave motion & senses. Bro. Odin, Loki
HONIR	m			Indecisiveness.
IDUN	f	BRAGI Ivuld 1		Spring. Immortal apples
KARI	m			Early god of air.
KVASIR(V)	m			Wisdom. Part Aesir
LODUR	m			Early god. Gave blood.
LOFN	f			Easing path of true and illicit love.
LOKI	m	SIGYN Thokk Angrboda	Sleipnir HEL f Fenrir Jormungland NARVI m VALI m	Lies, deceit, trickery and evil. Fire. After causing death of Balder he was bound beneath poison dripping snake.
MAGNI	m			Might.
MIMIR	m			Wisdom. Guards well.
MODI	m			Wrath
NAGLFARI	m	NOTT	AUD m	
NANNA	f	BALDER		
NARVI	m			Entrails bound Loki
NERTHUS(V)	f	NJORD	FREY m FREYJA f	Sea
NIGHT	f		NARVI	Night
NJORD(V)	m	NERTHUS SKALDI	FREYJA f Frey m	Sea
NORNS:				
SKULD	f			Fates: Being
URD	f			Fate
VERDANDI	f			Necessity
NOTT	f	NAGLFARI ANNAR DELLINGER	AUD m ERDA f DAG m	Night
OF	m	FREYJA	HNOSS f GERSEMI f	Left Freyja.
ODIN	m	FJORGYN FRIGGA RIND SAGA 1 Grid 1	THOR m BALDER m HODER m TYR m BRAGI m HEIMDALL m ULL m VIDAR m HERMOD m VALI m	Chief God - the All Father. Runes. A wide brimmed hat to shield a solitary eye. Many nick names. Ravens Huginn & Muginn. Wolves Freki & Gerinn. Spear Gugnir.
OSTARA	f			Spring
RAN	f	AEGIR	9 WAVE MAIDENS f	Sea. Net to pull down sailors. Sister as well as wife to Aegir.
RIND	f	ODIN	VALI m	Frozen soil, frigidity.
SAGA	f	ODIN 1		Stories
SATAERE	m			Agriculture

Name		Partner	Children	Description
SIF	f	THOR		Golden hair
		ODIN 1	ULL m	Ull by Odin
SIGURD	m	BRUNHILD		
		GUDRUN		
SIGYN	f	LOKI	NARVE m	Empties the bowl of
			VALI m	poison that drips onto Loki.
SKADI	f	NJORD		Snowshoes
SKALDI	f	ODIN 1		Poetry
SJOFN	f			Human passion
SNOTRA	f			Virtue. At. of Frigga
SUMMER	m			Summer
SVASUD	m		SUMMER m	Gentility
SYN	f			Trials
THOR	m	SIF		Thunder, law, fertility
		Iarnsaxa	MAGNI m	Hammer Mjollnir, plus
			MODI m	Grids belt of strength and gauntlets of iron. Goats Tanngnost and Tanngrisni pull chariot
TYR	m			War & Bravery. Lost his hand to monster wolf Fenrir.
ULL	m	SKADI		Winter, archery,
		FRIGGA 1		death, skiing. Glory.
VALI	m			To avenge death of Balder. Son of Odin and Rind. (Do not confuse with son of Loki)
VALI	m			Turned wolf to kill Narve (Son of Loki)
VALKIRIES	f			- see list at end
VARA	f			Oaths. Att. Frigga
VASUD	m		VINDSVAL m	Unfriendly,
VE	m	FRIGGA 1		Early god Bro. of Vili
VIDAR	m			Will slay Fenris and survive Ragnarok.
VILI	m	FRIGGA 1		Early god. Bro of Ve
VINDSVAL	m		WINTER m	Cold Wind
VJOFN	f			Conciliation Att. of Frigga
VOR	f			Faith. Knowledge of the future. Att. of Frigga
WINTER	m			Winter
WYRD	f			Mother of Norns.
VALKIRIES	f	All select slain for Valhalla - other details:		
ALVIT	f	A son of King Nidud		Allwise
AXE TIME	f			Mead bringer to Odin
BRUNHILD	f	SIGURD 1	Sigdrifa-	Victory giver
		GUTTORM		
GEIRAHOD	f			
GOLL	f			Screaming

88

Name			
GUDRUN	f	HELGI	
		SIGURD	
		ATLI	
GUNN	f		
GYNRITHA	f		
HERFJOTUR	f		Fetterer of an army
HILD	f		Battle
HLOKK	f		Shrieking
KIN OF THE GODS	f		
MIST	f		Mead bringer to Odin
OLRUN	f		A son of King Nidud
RADGRID	f		
RANDGRID	f		Shield destroyer
REGINLIEF	f		Conflict
ROTA a	f		
RUSILA	f		The Red Haired
SHAKER	f		Mead bringer to Odin
SHIELD BEARER	f		
SIGRUN	f	SVAVA f	
SKOGULL	f		Raging, Mead to Odin
SPEAR BEARER	f		
STICLA	f		
SVANHVIT	f	Married to a son of King Nidud	Swanwhite
THRUD	f		Din of battle
SVAVA	f		
SWANHILD f			
WARRIOR			
& MIGHT	f		
WRECKER OF			
PLANS	f		

Some Dwarf names AL, ALF, ALFRIG, ALTHJOF, ALVIS, ANDVARI, AURVANG,AUSTRI, BARI, BERLING, BROKK, DELLING, DOLGTHVARI, DORI, DRAUPNIR,DUF, DURIN, DVALIN, EIKINSKJALDI, EITRI, FAL, FROSTI, FID, FILI,FJALAR, FRAG, FRAR, FUNDIN, GALAR, GANDALF, GINNAR, GLOIN, GODAR,GRERR, HAR, HAUR, HEPTTIFILI, HLEDJOLF HORNBORI HUGSTARI, INGI,IRI, IVALDI, JARI, KILI, LIT, LONI, MODSOGNIR,MJODVITNIR, NIDI,NORDRI, NORI, NYI, NYR, NYRAD, OINN, ORI, RADSVID, REKK, SKAVIDSKIRFIR, SUDRI, SVIAR, SVIUR, THEKK, THORIN, THRAIN, THROR, UNI,VAR, VALI, VEGDRASIL, VIRFIR, VIT, VESTRI, VIG &VINDALF.

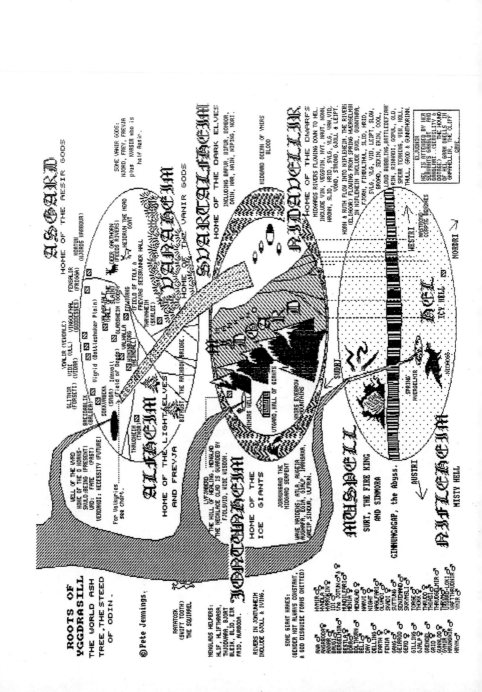

ROOTS OF YGGDRASILL
THE WORLD ASH TREE, THE STEED OF ODIN.

©Pete Jennings.

RATATOSK (SWIFT TOOTH) THE SQUIRREL.

ASGARD
HOME OF THE AESIR GODS

SOME VANIR GODS: NJORD, FREY, FREYJA plus KVASIR who is half Aesir.

WELL OF THE WYRD HOME OF THE NORNS-SKULD:BEING (PRESENT)
URD: FATE (PAST)
VERDANDI: NECESSITY (FUTURE)

For Valkyries see chart.

GLITNIR (FORSETI) VIDI (VIDAR) VINGOLF (GODDESSES) HORTUN (NJORDS HARBOUR)

VALA (VENDIR) VILI (ULL) FENSALIR (FRIGGA)

BREIDABLIK (BALDER) Vigrid (Battlefield Plain)

SOKKVABEKK Idavoll (Field of Deeds) GLADSHEIM (GODS) SAGA VALASKJALF Iceland (FEEDS RIVERS) SESSRUMNIR HALL FREYAS HEIDRUN THE HERD GOAT

VALHALLA THRYMHEIM (THOR) HIMINBJORG FOLKVANG (FIELD OF FOLK & THRYMHEIM (SKRLOI)

ALFHEIM
HOME OF THE LIGHT ELVES AND FREYJA

BIFROST, THE RAINBOW BRIDGE.

THE HILL LIFTHRASIR. HEMLIG THE NECKLACE CLAD IS GUARDED BY FJOLSVID. WIDE WISDOM.

VANIRS WELL

VANIRS EVEBROW MOUNTAINS

JOTUNHEIM
HOME OF THE ICE GIANTS

VANS, VAGGENS, ATLA, AUGEIA AIGIAFR, GINA, IARNSAXA, GREIP, SINDUR, ULFRUN.

JORUNGAND THE MIDGARD SERPENT

RIVERS IN JOTUNHEIM INCLUDE GJOLL & IVING.

(UTGARD, HALL OF GIANTS

VANAHEIM
HOME OF THE VANIR GODS

SVARTALFHEIM
HOME OF THE DARK ELVES

INCLUDING BAFUR, BIFUR, BONGOR, DAIN, NAR, NAIN, NIPING, NORI.

MIDGARD OCEAN OF YMIRS BLOOD

NIDAVELLIR
HOME OF THE DWARFS:

MIDGARDS RIVERS FLOWING DOWN TO HEL. INCLUDE VIN, VEGSVIN, NYT, NAUT, NONN, HRONN, SLID, HRID, SYLG, YLG, VAN, VID, VOND, STRAND, GJOLL & LEIPT.

HORN & RUTH FLOW INTO NIFLHEIM. THE RIVERS (ELIVAGR) FLOWING FROM SPRING HVERGELMIR IN NIFLHEIM INCLUDE SVOL, GUNTHRAA, FJORN, FIMBULTHAL, SLID, HRID, SYLG, YLG, VID, LEIPT, SLOW, BROAD, ZEVIN, EKIN, COOL, LOUD BUBBLING, BRITTLECREAMY RIN, RINANDI, GOPUL, OLD SPEER TEEMING, VIHI, HALL, THALL, GROO & GANTHRORIN.

ELIVODNIR
HEL IS INTENDED BY HER GRANDFATHER ODIN AND GANGLATI. (SERVILITY & DOTING) THE HOUND OF HEL, GARM DWELLS IN GNIPAHELLIR CAVE, THE CLIFF CAVE.

SUDRI

WESTRI

NORDRI

MISTRONG CORPSE BRIDGES

HEL
ICY HELL

SPRING HVERGELMIR

—NIDHOGG—

MUSPELL
SURT, THE FIRE KING AND SINMORA

GINNUNGAGAP, the Abyss.

AUSTRI

NIFLHEIM
MISTY HELL

SOME GIANT NAMES:
(GENDER NOT ALWAYS CONSTANT, A GOD DISGUISE FORMS OMITTED)

ANA ♂
ANGRBODA ♀
ANNAR ♂
BAUGI ♂
BERGELMIR ♂
BESTLA ♀
BOLTHORN ♂
DAY ♂
DELLING ♂
EARTH ♀
FENJA ♀
GANG ♂
GEIRROD ♂
GERD ♀
GILLING ♂
GJALP ♀
GRENDEL ♂
GRID ♀
GUNNLOD ♀
GYMIR ♂
HRYM ♂

HYMIR ♂
HYNDLA ♀
HYRROKIN ♀
IDI ♂
IM (JOTUN) ♂
IMD ♀
MIMIR ♂
MENJA ♀
MENGLAD ♀
NARVI ♂
NIGHT ♀
NINA/FRIGG ♀
OLVALDI ♂
SKADI ♀
SUTTUNG ♂
SENDIRMO ♂
SKRYMSLI ♂
TORGE ♂
THOKK ♀
THIAZI ♂
THJODR ♂
THRUDGELMIR ♂
URDUR-LONI ♂
VAFTHRUDNIR ♂

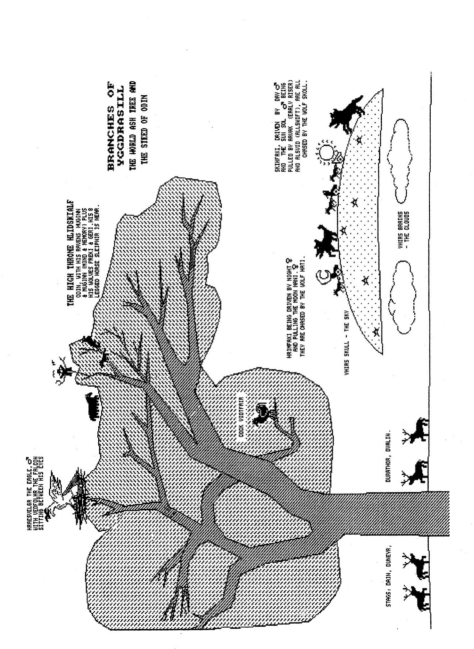

BRANCHES OF YGGDRASILL
THE WORLD ASH TREE AND
THE STEED OF ODIN

THE HIGH THRONE HLIDSKJALF
ODIN, WITH HIS RAVENS HUGINN
& MUGINN (MIND & MEMORY) PLUS
HIS WOLVES FREKI & GERI. HIS 8
LEGGED HORSE SLEIPNIR IS NEAR.

HRAESVELGR THE EAGLE, ♂
WITH VEDFOLNIR THE FALCON
SITTING BETWEEN HIS EYES

COCK VIDTFAIR

SKINFAXI, DRIVEN BY DAY ♂
AND THE SUN SOL, ♂ BEING
PULLED BY ARVAK (EARLY RISER)
AND ALSVID (ALLSWIFT), ARE ALL
CHASED BY THE WOLF SKOLL.

HRIMFAXI BEING DRIVEN BY NIGHT ♀
AND PULLING THE MOON MANI ♂
THEY ARE CHASED BY THE WOLF HATI.

YMIRS SKULL - THE SKY

YMIRS BRAINS
- THE CLOUDS

DURATHOR, DVALIN.

STAGS: DAIN, DUNEYR,

PATH No. 32

Since the original edition of this book was published, one or two readers have responded by writing in with paths that they have made. We would like to finish this chapter with a couple, and invite you to send in yours for a possible inclusion in a further volume of this book. The address is at the back under 'IpswichPathworking Group'. This path is by Carol Willis.

(1)　　　You are standing in front of a large stone staircase. The bottom step stretches to either side of you as far as your eyes can see. As you step onto it feel it's age and strength. Your feet feel cooler as they contact the stone. Step two is ahead of you, step onto it and feel more confident. Step three, and now you can see the edges of the stair several metres away to either side of you. Step four, and the ground behind you seems far away. Step five, the coldness of the stone is comforting and gives you the strength to continue upwards. Step six, and you notice the stairs are narrowing to form a point above you. Step seven and the world behind you seems vaguer now, step eight and you see an opening a few steps above you. Step nine, the opening is round, shaped like an open eye, it is just one step above you. Step ten, you have reached the eye, the stairs continuing past it above you getting forever narrower. Stop here where it is safe. Now step through the dark pupil and into another world.

(2a)　　　In front of you is a green grassy hill with a sandy path where others have climbed it in the past. The sun shines over the crest, and there is a shape silhouetted just below the top of the hill. It is hard to be certain what it is from here, so knowing you are safe here, follow the path in front of you to find out who or what is waiting for you at the top......

(2b)　　　It is time to move on now, so say your farewells and turn to look around. In the distance you can see a beautiful lake. It's surrounded by trees and the waters look clear and inviting. Leave your worries behind you and step out onto the air away from the hill. Let yourself be lifted off the ground and carried by the sky towards this lake. Take your time and enjoy the sensation of floating. It is a very sensual feeling, and you are free from all the normal restraints. Drift slowly towards your target.........

(3)   From up here the lake looks even more enticing. Drift slowly down until you feel safe, then let yourself drop into the centre of the lake. Enjoy the splash you make and let the waters take you deeper. Feel the cool clean water all around you. Let it wash you and leave you cooler, and clearer.....

(2c)   Surface again and look around you. The lake is surrounded by trees with several small clearings along the waters edge. In one of them a small fire burns. You are free and totally safe. None can come here without your invitation, so stay for a while and enjoy your surroundings....

(4)   You see the fire in your clearing has almost burnt out, and it is time for you to go back. Look into the fire and see your own eye reflected back at you. Concentrate and it grows, leaving the fire behind. Watch quietly until it is the size you remember coming through......Now step back through the eye and onto the stone pyramid. 10, and you're back on the stone. 9, you've left the other world behind but not forgotten it. 8, 7, 6, you are moving back down the stairs feeling safe and secure as you approach the ground. 5, you are half way there, 4, 3, the stairs behind you begin to fade. 2, you can see the ground, 1 you step onto the ground and leave the stairs to fade. In their place is the room you started from. When you are ready open your eyes.

PATH No. 33

I identify very strongly with the Green Man, so was delighted to be able to use this pathworking by Mick Galvin.

(1)   The group leader prepares the group by relaxing them in a quiet, relaxed atmosphere, and a member of the group reads the following poem:

The Green Man
Pagan symbol of nature, fertility and rebirth.
Spirit guardian of the forests,
Know him as Jack of the Green
Robin of the Wood, Green George, The Burry Man
And by his many other guises.
Perhaps as important today in the times
Of pollution, destruction and waste
As he ever was.
Look for him in the countryside
In churches, festivals, and old buildings.
Look for him as you walk the woods and lanes.
Look for him in your heart
And you will find him.

After visualising a protective circle of light, the group leader starts to 'bring down' the group into a state of relaxation for pathworking. When the whole group is ready, begin. You are walking along the edge of a huge forest, and to the right of you is an enormous ploughed field that sweeps down and away over the horizon. The sun is setting and everything is coloured a deep red hue, the air is warm and still and you can smell the freshly turned earth.

You wander along the side of the mass of leaves and branches seeking and searching until suddenly you find a slight gap, like a small doorway in the thick foliage, and somehow you know that this is meant for you. For a moment you hesitate, then you duck your head and slowly enter.

From the warm crimson light of the outside you now enter a world of green shades and shadows, birds sing and insects dance around your head. The trees soar high above like Gothic pillars and form a roof-like canopy of leaves where small beams of light filter down, cutting through the haze and illuminating where they fall.

(3)   There is a small stream at your feet, laughing and bubbling it entices you to follow as it meanders by and away. You walk forwards, deeper and deeper into the green mass, the smells of pine and other woods pervade your senses, and the ferns and soft mushy mosses comfort your tired feet, for you have travelled a long way to reach this place. The whole forest seems alive, it seems to breath and sigh with a deep intensity, the rustling of a lost breeze sending wave like ripples across an ocean of bluebells that greet you as you enter a clearing.

(2)   To your right is a small but definite path, the earth hardened by footsteps over the ages, you follow the path deeper and deeper into the heart of the forest, small animals rustle the bushes and dart away. As you pass near larger animals to avoid your presence, you are not here to meet them.

You have travelled far by now and you are feeling tired, but as if in acknowledgement of this you suddenly realise you have reached your goal. This is a special place. A ring of huge, gnarled oaks ancient and grey against the green around them, their branches like talons or fingers twisting and joining into a maze of wood. You pause and then enter the circle, and immediately know this is a sacred space. The air is different here, the noise of the forest dies, but you feel the energy pulsating, driving you in.

You find your spot and sit and wait, closing your eyes you meditate on why you are here. Time passes and there is a strange tension in the air, your senses alive and alert. How long you sit you do not know, but you suddenly hear a crack of twig and heavy footsteps, slow and lumbering, the leaves and bracken crackling as he comes. It is the Green Man. You open your eyes and he stands before you as old as time, the Green God, awesome and magnificent, towering and terrifying, but you are not afraid. You are Pagan, and he is a Pagan God, you are as one, and he has come to you. You ask him what you need to know, and he will tell you what you need to hear. As you sit together I will leave you for a while......

(4)   It is time now - you thank him, close your eyes again and listen as the Green Man leaves you, back into the Wild Wood until he is summoned again. Armed with your knowledge and in your own time leave the circle and follow the path back to the stream, and out of the forest into the ploughed field. It is night now. There is a full moon and the countryside and hills are illuminated with a silver light. As you leave an owl hoots and a cock pheasant cackles farewell from deep inside the wood. You wander back from whence you came. Slowly and in your own time awake back into consciousness... In your own time.....

PATH No. 34

This last path has one of the most original opening sequences I have seen in a long time. It just goes to prove that when you think that all the possible alternatives have been exhausted, along comes another. It was put together by Lee Wyatt.

(1)   After getting comfy and relaxed, you see that you are in a big room. Just a nice, cosy room. There is a roaring fire in the hearth. Before you on the table are ten small leather pouches. You pick up the first and open it. You then empty the contents into your hand. You are holding a fine coloured powder, which you toss into the air beside you. It lingers and floats in the air....... Now do the same with the 2nd pouch...and the 3rd, 4th, 5th, 6th, 7th, 8th, 9th and 10th..

(3)   You come out of the colour into a large meadow. You are surrounded by green grass, yellow flowers and white blooms. The sun is warm on your face, and there are no clouds in the sky. In the distance you can see a lush, green forest. You head for that forest........

(2a)   As you near the forest you can see on it's edge a group of small cottages. As you near these cottages you can smell cooking and hear the sound of music and singing.......

(2b)   It is time to leave the festivities now, time to head into the forest. After walking a short way into the forest you see a dark robed and hooded figure beckoning you as you approach. He asks you to follow him. You may speak to him...

(2c)   After a time you arrive at a ruined castle. The figure bids you enter. Through the doorway you enter a large room. Sitting cross legged on the floor is someone you know very well. The person motions you to sit down. You sit down and watch as the figure builds a small fire. As the fire burns the figure motions you to look into the flames. As you look into the flames a question is answered and you feel a great weight off your mind...........

(4)   The figure bids you farewell and you start to walk back through the forest. You will walk past the village until you come to your gateway of coloured dust. You step through and find yourself back in the small wooden room, and start to gather the dust. You wave your hand into the dust and fill your first bag. You do the same with the 2nd, 3rd, 4th, 5th, 6th, 7th, 8th, 9th and 10th, coming back to reality as you do so.

9. SOME CONCLUSIONS AND WHERE TO GO FROM HERE

So, you have worked your way through the book and wondering "What next?" You are not alone, so are we! Seriously though, a book like this tends to raise as many questions as it answers. The biggest question is does it work, and if so, how? Well, it seems to work for us and many others, but as to how, that is another question. I have heard theories of mild hypnosis, of a triggering of the natural dream mechanism, and of it being solely the fevered imagination of the subject at work. All, or none of these theories could be correct, along with many others including Out Of Body experiences, astral travelling or e.s.p. We as authors do not claim the divine knowledge of which theory is right, and do not believe it is our place to do so. Despite the advances in modern medical science, the worlds top physicians still admit there are huge gaps in their knowledge in the workings of the brain. They know it is a million times more powerful that the mightiest computer, and that it constantly readjusts itself to allow for new information being taken in. They know that certain areas are responsible for particular activities, but there are others which as yet are unfathomed.

So medically, what do we know? Well, to start with, it is generally accepted that passive relaxation, whether just sitting down looking out of the window or doing yoga, tends to lower the pulse rate and blood pressure. You might like to take pulse rates before and after a session of pathworking, to try and measure effectiveness for yourself. If one of your number is of the medical fraternity, you could even get some blood pressure readings as well. As I have said before, we are not medical experts, but I would be interested to see if the brainwave patterns resemble states of hypnosis, sleep, transcendental meditation etc. As our health services get stretched, surely a bit of simple research into a very cheap, safe alternative to drugs would be worthwhile? The opinions of people like ourselves, however genuine, cannot be regarded as subjective. We have a vested interest in wanting what we do to be seen as effective, so however much we might maintain it relaxes us, heals us or solves our practical and psychological problems, the convincing proof needs to come from the scientific community. It is because of their recognised impartiality that I believe we should strive harder for their acceptance, and in doing so maybe find some of the answers we cannot provide ourselves. It may be that they are not able to find out how it works, no more than we, but they just might as in many other fields be able to measure effect without knowing the cause.

So how else can you develop your new found skills? Well, inevitably, some of the pathworkings will cause you to question your religious beliefs, whatever they might be. That is surely a good thing, because a religion that cannot withstand healthy questioning must be too dogmatic. It is not for us to say where this should lead you, but if it causes you to consider one of the branches of Paganism, we have included some contact addresses in the back of this book. We reckon all the other main religions can be found in the telephone book!

Additionally, you might become interested in healing via pathworking methods. Virtually all cultures throughout the world have had shamanistic healers, using pathworking methods. The similarity between their working practices are remarkable, considering they may be in places as far apart as North and South America, Africa, Greenland and Australia. It is very difficult for anyone in our urbanised modern society to become fully shamanistic, but it is conceivable for some of their methods to be imitated, despite differing religious or cultural beliefs.

Of course, modern psychiatry frequently uses role playing methods to enable patients to reconstruct problem situations and resolve them. Other physicians are using bio feedback techniques to enable patients to positively think their way towards pain relief and immune systems. You may feel the value of this element of pathworking could be exploited, although of course you must not tread into medical or social work territory whilst inexperienced or unqualified. I do find it amusing though that the more that medical science develops non-intrusive methods, the more they appear to resemble the old medicine man or womans ways! Once again though I would caution against making wild unsubstantiated ways for pathworking methods. You should have found out by now that they only work for people open minded enough to allow them to work within them. Some people are not capable of allowing that to happen to them. Even people who do regularly pathwork are unable to benefit sometimes when they feel 'blocked' by the residue of a hectic or disruptive day. Maybe your experiences within pathworking will lead you to be interested in working for the caring services, whether that be in medicine or social work. It would be good to see more of our methods incorporated into the mainstream. It will be a long job though. Think how long it has taken for the once scorned science of acupuncture to become accepted. One is encouraged to hear of doctors and midwives in some places encouraging patients to get themselves a meditation tape to relax with. From such small acorns do mighty oak trees grow!

We hope this book is a sort of acorn as well. We would be interested to hear your opinions and experiences with it. A contact address can be found on page 103, under Ipswich Pathworking Group. One day we hope to develop a further book of advanced paths, and we are not too proud to accept some that others have come up with, so do send us those as well!

Finally, a look at what you should have learnt, and some advice. You should by now have a pretty good idea of what pathworking (also called channelling and questing) is. Do not be blinkered though, as it means many things to different people. It may even with time and effort come to mean different things to you. You should have learnt it is no good rushing the preparations and the steps to go down. Without these being effective, all other effort is wasted. Plan the four or more stages beforehand, and try and stick to the plan. Afterwards, enjoy the analysis and discussion. This should be a pleasurable exchange between like minded people. If it is not, did you learn the lessons of forming a group properly? Or have you rushed onto advanced paths without giving everyone a chance to reach a reasonable level of confidence with simpler workings. If you are not enjoying it, you are not doing it right!

BIBLIOGRAPHY AND CONTACT ADDRESSES

The following books and magazines may be of interest for readers to expand their knowledge on particular topics mentioned within this book. They are merely a starting point, and many have extensive bibliographies of their own. Information is correct at the time of going to press, but we take no responsibility for subsequent changes in situation. Most magazines will send you a sample copy for £1.50, and subscription to one with an address near you will often bring local contacts and information. We have given a comprehensive list of magazines also because they keep you in touch via their reviews of the latest books, events, organisations etc. long after we have gone to press.

Ace of Rods (Contact mag.) BCM Akademia, London WCl 3XX
Advanced Magical Arts. R.J. Stewart. (Element)
Albion, Pete Ricketts, 43, Rowley St Walsall WS1 2AX
A Separate Reality. Carlos Castaneda (Bodley Head)
ASH (general mag) 2, Kent View Rd., Vange, Basildon, Essex.
Bridestone (formerly Unicorn) PO Box 18, Hessle E. Yorks.
Cauldron (general mag) Caemorgan Cottage, Caemorgan Rd., Cardigan, Dyfed, Wales.
Challice, 16 Blenheim Rd., Beechwood, Newport, Gwent Wales.
Chaos International BM Sorcery, London WClN 3XX
Dalriada, Dun-na-Beatha, 2 Brathwic Place, Brodick, Isle of Arran, Scotland KA27 8BN
Deosil Dance. Magazine plus other books BCM Pentacle, London WC1N 3XX
Dragons Brew, C. Breen, 50 Hookland Rd, Porthcawl, Mid Glam.
Earthworks, 145 Ketts Hill, Norwich NRl 4HD
The Elements of Visualisation Ursula Markham (Elements)
Foresight, 44 Brockhurst Rd, Hodge Hill Birmingham B36 8JB
Gates of Annwn, (contact mag.) BM Gates of Annwn, London WCl
Gippeswic (Mag. edited by Pete Jennings) 42 Cemetery Rd, Ipswich, Suffolk IP4 2JA.
Gnosis, Cthonios Books, 7 Tamarisk Steps, Hastings Sussex

Gods & Heroes from Viking Mythology. Brian Branston (Book Club Associates)

Golden Bough. J.G. Fraser (Papermac)

Green Circle (organisation) PO BOX 42, Bath BA1 1ZN

Greenleaf (Festival & New Age newsletter). 96, Church St., Redfield, Bristol.

Hammer of the North Magnus Magnusson (Book Club Associates)

Insight, 25, Calmore Close, Bournemouth, Dorset BH8 0NN

Ipswich Pathworking Group, c/o 42, Cemetery Rd., Ipswich, Suffolk. IP4 2JA

Isian News (Fellowship of Isis) Clonegal Castle, Enniscorthy Eire

Journey to Ixtlan. Carlos Castaneda (Bodley Head)

Kabbalist, 25 Circlew Gardens, London SW19 3JX

Kallisti (Chaos) PO Box 57, Norwich NR2 2RX

Lamp of Thoth, 31 Kings Ave, Leeds 6

Leaves of Yggdrasil Freya Aswynn (Llewellyn)

London Earth Mysteries Circle, (Lecture organisation) 18, Christchurch Ave, London NW6

Magonia, John Dee Cott, 5 James Terrace, London SW14 8HB

Medicine Ways (Shamanism mag.) Galdraheim, 35, Wilson Ave., Deal, Kent.

Mercian Mysteries, 2 Cross Hill Close, Wymeswold Loughborough, LE12 6UJ

Meyn Mamvro (Cornish) 52 Caren Bosavern, St Just, Penzance Cornwall TR19 7QX

Moonshine BM Moonstone London WC1 3XX

Moonstone (general mag.) BM Moonstone London WC1 3XX

New Dimensions, Dept 10, 1 Austin Close, Irchester Northants

Norse Myths Kevin Crossley-Holland (Penguin)

Nuit Isis (Golden Dawn) PO Box 250 Oxford OX1 1AP

*Occult Observer, Atlantis Bookshop, 49a Museum St London WC1

Odalstone (mag of Odinshof) BCM Tercel London WC1 3XX

Odinisn Today (mag of Odinic Rite) BM Edda, London WC1 3XX

Paganlink, (contact organisation) National Clearing House, 25, East Hill, Dartford, Kent DA1 1RX

Pagan Life Bridge House, Clonegal, Enniscorthy Co. Wexford Eire

Pagan News PO Box 196 London WC1A 2DY

Pagan Voice, 13 Barnstaple Walk, Knowle, Bristol BS4 1JQ

Pandoras Jar (ex Pipes of Pan) Blaenberem, Mynyddcerrig, Llanelli, Dyfed Cymru SAl5 5BL

Path, 97 Alrewas Rd, Kings Bromley, Staffs DEl3 7HR

Practical Magic in the Northern Tradition Nigel Pennick (Aquarian)

Prediction (general mag., available on major bookstalls) Link House, Dingwall Ave., Croydon, Surrey. CR9 2TA

Quest (general mag.) BCM SCL Quest, London WCl 3XX

Rites of Odin. Ed Fitch (Llewellyn)

Real Magic. Isaac Bonewits (Weiser)

Ritual Magic Workbook: Dolores Ashcroft-Nowicki (Aquarian)

Secret Law of Runes & Other Ancient Alphabets. Nigel Pennick (Rider)

Silver Moon, Response, 300 Old Brompton Rd, London SW5 9JF

Silver Wheel (Celtic mag.) Anna Franklin, Windrush, High Tor West, Earl Shilton, Leics.

Sirius (Mag. of Fellowship of Isis) Ida Publications, PO Box 428, Denbigh, Clwyd, N. Wales LLl6 4AZ.

*Skoob, Skoob Books, 15 Sicilian Ave, London WClA 2QH

Sut Anubis, Occultique 73 Kettering Rd, Northampton.

Sword of Wayland, Geoff Dunn, Bryn Aber, Fairy Glen Rd, Dwygy Fychi, Penmaenawr, Gwynedd LL34 6YU

Talking Stick (Magazine and lecture group.) Suite B, 2, Tunstall Rd., London SW9 8DA

The Teachings of Don Juan. Carlos Castaneda (Bodley Head)

Touchwood (general mag.) PO Box 36, Whitley Bay, Tyne & Wear

Valknut, Hardrada, 9 Stour Rd, Crayford Kent DAl 4PJ

Viking Mythology John Grant (Quintet)

The Viking Gods Clive Barrett (Aquarian)

The Way of the Shaman: Michael Harner. (Bantam New Age)

The Way of the Wyrd: Brian Bates. (Century Publishing)

The Wiccan (Mag. of Pagan Federation who act as a contact and information umbrella organisation) BM Box 7097, London

*The two addresses marked thus are also bookshops who specialise in esoteric subjects.

Pete Jennings has a further book being issued soon, called "Singing East Anglia", published by Brewhouse, about the folklore and songs of East Anglia.

Practical Spirituality by Steve Hounsome

Many people today struggle with attempting to blend a spiritual life with the demands of work, home and family. For many, the rampant commercialism, exploitation and consequent destruction of the modern 'developed' world is in direct conflict with the sacred ideals held so dear by those who seek to live the way of the spirit. This book addresses this problem, offering a means whereby the dedicated, serious practitioner can learn to live a practical, spiritual life, with what is sacred to them at its heart and as its focus. This is achieved by close association with the natural world, the wheel of nature round its annual cycle and the Elements that constitute its life. There are many practical exercises included to help you find your way.

ISBN 186163 015 8 £10.95   **R97**   Illustrated

Practical Meditation by Steve Hounsome

A truly practical book which assists us to learn to use meditation in our daily lives, to help reduce tension and promote better reactions in mind and body. "Practical Meditation" separates meditation techniques into easily defined areas, such as breathing exercises, relaxation techniques and healing meditations and there is a full section on learning to "ground" oneself so that the reader can keep their feet firmly on the ground and functioning to their best in the everyday world. The book aims to take the mystery out of meditation, making this ancient practice available to an ever widening group of people. The meditations are explained in terms which are easy to understand and are written for people from all walks of life who are showing an increased interest in meditation.

ISBN 1898307 58X   £10.95   Illustrated

The Intuitive Journey by Ann Walker

The journey in this book is, of course, the one from birth to death. During the course of a lifetime we have many different bodies, differing in size and appearance, yet our inner view of ourselves may change little from childhood to old age. Much has been written about developing psychic powers. The author sets out to prove that it is not a question of a favoured few developing special qualities, but of removing the blocks to using the gifts each one of us has been given to help us on what should, indeed be an intuitive journey.

ISBN 1898307 865   £8.95

Mind Massage by Marlene E Maundrill

Sixty Creative Visualisations to Bring Calm, Relaxation and Tranquillity Into Your Life

Many people have learnt to relax using tapes - words and music. For groups, or yourself, this book gives an opportunity to read aloud and/or tape, in your own special voice, inspiring and relaxing visualisations. These can benefit in many ways - reducing stress or blood pressure, pain clinics, hyperactivity in children, a tape of a beloved voice giving company and healing for those in hospital or hospice. After more than 20 years of this work, Marlene continues to lead groups and offers therapy to those in need - including Past Life Therapy, using her psychic awareness to channel. Everyone is able to do this work, the words in this book form the stepping stones across the first barrier to release your own answers and your own abilities.

ISBN 186163 005 0£9.95   **R97**   Illustrated

FREE DETAILED CATALOGUE

A detailed illustrated catalogue is available on request, SAE or International Postal Coupon appreciated. Titles are available direct from Capall Bann, post free in the UK (cheque or PO with order) or from good bookshops and specialist outlets. Titles currently available include:

Animals, Mind Body Spirit & Folklore

Angels and Goddesses - Celtic Christianity & Paganism by Michael Howard
Arthur - The Legend Unveiled by C Johnson & E Lung
Auguries and Omens - The Magical Lore of Birds by Yvonne Aburrow
Book of the Veil The by Peter Paddon
Caer Sidhe - Celtic Astrology and Astronomy by Michael Bayley
Call of the Horned Piper by Nigel Jackson
Cats' Company by Ann Walker
Celtic Lore & Druidic Ritual by Rhiannon Ryall
Compleat Vampyre - The Vampyre Shaman: Werewolves & Witchery by Nigel Jackson
Crystal Clear - A Guide to Quartz Crystal by Jennifer Dent
Earth Dance - A Year of Pagan Rituals by Jan Brodie
Earth Harmony - Places of Power, Holiness and Healing by Nigel Pennick
Earth Magic by Margaret McArthur
Enchanted Forest - The Magical Lore of Trees by Yvonne Aburrow
Familiars - Animal Powers of Britain by Anna Franklin
Healing Homes by Jennifer Dent
Herbcraft - Shamanic & Ritual Use of Herbs by Susan Lavender & Anna Franklin
In Search of Herne the Hunter by Eric Fitch
Inner Space Workbook - Developing Counselling & Magical Skills Through the Tarot
Kecks, Keddles & Kesh by Michael Bayley
Living Tarot by Ann Walker
Magical Incenses and Perfumes by Jan Brodie
Magical Lore of Cats by Marion Davies
Magical Lore of Herbs by Marion Davies
Masks of Misrule - The Horned God & His Cult in Europe by Nigel Jackson
Mysteries of the Runes by Michael Howard
Oracle of Geomancy by Nigel Pennick
Patchwork of Magic by Julia Day
Pathworking - A Practical Book of Guided Meditations by Pete Jennings
Pickingill Papers - The Origins of Gardnerian Wicca by Michael Howard
Psychic Animals by Dennis Bardens
Psychic Self Defence - Real Solutions by Jan Brodie
Runic Astrology by Nigel Pennick
Sacred Animals by Gordon MacLellan
Sacred Grove - The Mysteries of the Forest by Yvonne Aburrow
Sacred Geometry by Nigel Pennick
Sacred Lore of Horses The by Marion Davies
Sacred Ring - Pagan Origins British Folk Festivals & Customs by Michael Howard
Seasonal Magic - Diary of a Village Witch by Paddy Slade
Secret Places of the Goddess by Philip Heselton
Talking to the Earth by Gordon Maclellan
Taming the Wolf - Full Moon Meditations by Steve Hounsome
The Goddess Year by Nigel Pennick & Helen Field
West Country Wicca by Rhiannon Ryall
Witches of Oz The by Matthew & Julia Phillips

Capall Bann is owned and run by people actively involved in many of the areas in which we publish. Our list is expanding rapidly so do contact us for details on the latest releases.

Capall Bann Publishing, Freshfields, Chieveley, Berks, RG20 8TF